C000091739

A Teacher's Guide
to Musical Theatre

David Henson is Associate Professor of Performance and former Director at London College of Music with skills in directing, acting and musical theatre. He is currently researching for a book publication on dialogue in the performance space. He has been responsible for creating postgraduate and undergraduate courses in Acting, Musical Theatre, Voice Studies, Acting & Theatre Making and Actor Musicianship courses in many conservatoires and universities, including the Royal Central School of Speech and Drama. He is creator and writer of First Advanced Level Performing Arts and Chief Examiner for Advanced Level Music, Drama and Performing Arts plus vocational qualifications at all levels. He is also author of three publications in musical theatre and has recently completed a chapter in Bloomsbury's Perspectives and Practices in Popular Music Education.

Kenneth Pickering is currently Hon. Professor of Drama at the University of Kent and lead assessor for the Council for Dance, Drama and Musical Theatre. He is former Professor of Theatre at Gonzaga University, USA and Chief Examiner for Speech, Drama and Musical Theatre for the London College of Music and Trinity/Guildhall. He is consultant to Rock School and Stagecoach Theatre Schools. He is author of thirteen published and widely performed plays and musicals, as well as the books *Studying Modern Drama*, *Key Concepts in Drama and Performance*, *Drama Improvised* and *Drama in the Cathedral*, and co-author of *Theatre Studies*, *Naturalism in Theatre*, *Choreographing the Stage Musical* and two Workbooks for Musical Theatre (with David Henson). He has recently completed a chapter on Peter Brook for Bloomsbury.

A Teacher's Guide to Musical Theatre

Kenneth Pickering
and
David Henson

methuen | drama
LONDON · NEW YORK · OXFORD · NEW DELHI · SYDNEY

METHUEN DRAMA
Bloomsbury Publishing Plc
50 Bedford Square, London, WC1B 3DP, UK
1385 Broadway, New York, NY 10018, USA
29 Earlsfort Terrace, Dublin 2, Ireland

BLOOMSBURY, METHUEN DRAMA and the Methuen Drama logo are trademarks of
Bloomsbury Publishing Plc

First published in Great Britain 2021

Copyright © Kenneth Pickering and David Henson, 2021

Kenneth Pickering and David Henson have asserted their right under the Copyright,
Designs and Patents Act, 1988, to be identified as authors of this work.

For legal purposes the Acknowledgements on p. vii constitute an extension
of this copyright page.

Cover design: Rebecca Heselton

All rights reserved. No part of this publication may be reproduced or transmitted
in any form or by any means, electronic or mechanical, including photocopying,
recording, or any information storage or retrieval system, without prior
permission in writing from the publishers.

Bloomsbury Publishing Plc does not have any control over, or responsibility for,
any third-party websites referred to or in this book. All internet addresses given
in this book were correct at the time of going to press. The author and publisher
regret any inconvenience caused if addresses have changed or sites have
ceased to exist, but can accept no responsibility for any such changes.

A catalogue record for this book is available from the British Library.

ISBN: HB: 978-1-3502-1393-7
        PB: 978-1-3502-1392-0
        ePDF: 978-1-3502-1394-4
        eBook: 978-1-3502-1395-1

Typeset by RefineCatch Limited, Bungay, Suffolk
Printed and bound in Great Britain

To find out more about our authors and books visit www.bloomsbury.com
and sign up for our newsletters.

CONTENTS

ACKNOWLEDGEMENTS

The authors wish to express their warmest thanks to: Professor John Caputo at Gonzaga University for his initial guidance; Louise Lewis for her helpful research; Professor Kevin Landis and Solveig Olsen at the University of Colorado, Colorado Springs, Associate Professor Laura Wayth at San Francisco State University, Charlie Gilbert with his brilliant SAVI project and Suzie J. Jarmain at Monash University for their inspiration and help; colleagues and friends at the Council for Dance, Drama and Musical Theatre and their accredited Colleges and Ian Duguid and Emma Evans at The London College of Music for opportunities to observe and discuss the teaching of musical theatre; Andrew Smith for help with transcribing musical scores; David Burridge and Martin Riley for permission to use *The Burning of the Boats*; Charlotte Emmett for her careful work on the MS and our Editor at Bloomsbury/Methuen, Don O'Hanlon for believing in our work.

KP and DH

Introduction

'Beyond the Notes'

this competitor took us far beyond the notes
COMMENTARY ON BBC YOUNG MUSICIAN OF THE YEAR COMPETITION

This book is written to support the work of teachers and instructors in Musical Theatre at College or University level. It envisages an initial one term or semester 'Introduction to Musical Theatre' which involves approximately three hours a week of class time. However, it establishes principles and suggested techniques of teaching which remain valid for work at more advanced levels. We assume that students will have enrolled on your course of study for a variety of reasons, ranging from a fascination with a popular form of entertainment to a wish to enter the highly demanding and competitive field of professional Theatre. Accordingly, we are assuming that they will bring a wide variety of abilities and experience to their studies. Furthermore, we are convinced that none of them will achieve anything of worth unless they **understand the principles** which lie behind every work and performance of Musical Theatre. We also assume that **you** will bring very diverse expertise and understanding to the work but that you are willing to work together with other teachers and practitioners and learn to widen your horizons rather than cling stubbornly to what you already know!

Why study Musical Theatre?

Theatre which combines acting, dancing, singing, design, poetry, dialogue and storytelling appears to have its roots in several ancient civilizations and that alone makes it worth studying. However, since the early years of the twentieth century, an art form that originated in Europe and the United States, and was popularized to a large extent through recorded media, has become a major global commodity and a phenomenon that demands investigation. Growing out of operetta and originally termed 'Musical Comedy', the 'Musical' has developed into a sophisticated genre capable of dealing memorably with almost every aspect of the human condition and it has come to dominate the theatres of most major cities and towns in the world. Musicals have a huge presence on screen and thus can be experienced in every corner of the world. Both professional and community productions of Musicals now form the majority of Theatre performances in many cultural centres and the skills required to participate seem to grow ever more varied and sophisticated. Your students must be made aware that **an understanding of Musical Theatre requires a huge range of critical and performance skills.** It is our job to help them to realize this from the outset, even if their ambition is simply to take the first steps.

Beyond the notes

Our approach to helping you to become an effective teacher of Musical Theatre depends on our conviction that talent shows and the recorded media have made it far too easy for students to imagine that by an enthusiastic imitation of a favourite performance they, themselves, can become expert performers. There is an equal, and even more fundamentally dishonest, belief that a few hours a week of study can in some way prepare students for professional performance. So you will see how important it is to use a programme of study such as we are suggesting to **establish the principles** before there is any thought of making a career out of Musical Theatre. The first principle is that the reproduction of a song, dance or piece of dialogue must **always** be rooted in an understanding of the context and motivation of the piece and must go far beyond singing the right notes, speaking the right words or mastering the right dance steps. You will notice that we do not hesitate to suggest that you find ways of imparting information because we believe that knowledge leads to understanding and that understanding leads to greater enjoyment.

Integration or disintegration

Imagine this scenario:

A Contemporary Dancer has joined your staff and decides to make a dance entitled 'Katyn' with your students. She has recently returned with her company from a tour of Poland, where the dance was first performed. She is not too sure why the accompanying music is by Chopin nor precisely why the piece is entitled 'Katyn'.

Yes, we have all been there: the accompanist who says it is his or her job to simply 'play the dots', the designer who creates a ramp on which no actor or dancer can stand, the costume designer who creates hats for the chorus which make physical movement impossible, the choreographer who thinks that a sequence learned on a cruise ship is ideal for your show, the singing teacher who tacks on a few gestures and calls it 'acting', the drama teacher who doesn't listen to the music . . . **and yet** it is precisely in making connections that we give the study of Musical Theatre the artistic and academic integrity to justify its inclusion as a subject at University or College.

It was probably in the early years of the twentieth century that there were conscious efforts by Theatre thinkers to explore common ground in the arts. This has led to plenty of lively debates and experiments and has culminated in attempts to integrate the teaching of performing arts in very exciting ways. This is not always easy because it demands much more than co-operation (although that is a good and sadly rare start!) but involves a true understanding of the dynamic and rich relationships between various modes of performance. For example, one College catalogue of courses made the following statement in the late twentieth century: 'students will discover how traditional boundaries between "subjects" will collapse and disappear.' Our experience shows that this is an aim which is yet to be achieved in many cases, but it is our belief that the exploration of the boundaries and the ability to make connections is what we should be asking of our students and of ourselves. If you feel that being asked to co-operate with and understand the concerns of other Theatre artists is a recent issue, please remember that as long ago as 1889 the Theatre impresario Augustus Harris was writing:

> A spectacular theatre must be . . . the trysting place (i.e. meeting place) of all the arts. The work itself must be a labour of love, of perseverance, and of pluck: the co-operation of the most accomplished masters of the various arts should be secured.
>
> RICHARDS, 2015

Using this book

The 'lessons' contained in this book provide structure, suggested content and underlying principles for your teaching. They offer a programme of work which can engage students for a term, a semester or even a year and inspire them to take their studies further. However, any one of these lessons can be expanded to form a major project demanding personal research, substantial rehearsal and preparation by your students as well as leading to performances of ever-increasing ambition and complexity. In all aspects of the suggested activities we would recommend a constant emphasis on rigour: ensuring that the creators of works are correctly acknowledged and that both research and the development of skills are an exercise in self-monitoring. We would also strongly advise you to look upon your 'casting' of roles within the work as an opportunity to explore both ethnic and gender diversity. You will find that Musical Theatre is a particularly rich field for the application of such issues in a sensitively managed way.

How you decide to use the book, therefore, is a matter of personal choice and need but we hope that it establishes principles and ways of working that remain with you throughout your teaching career. You will also need to decide on the best way in which to introduce musical examples: you may have good keyboard or vocal skills and demand 'live' work of yourself and your students, but you and your students now have almost limitless access to recorded material that can be made instantly available. If the use of recordings is your chosen method, we would urge you to insist that students not only hear the musical examples but actually **listen** to music in a way to which they may not be accustomed.

We wish you well in your work.

Lesson One

The Elements of Musical Theatre

Lesson themes

Students electing to study Musical Theatre often think that this experience will simply be an extension of their High School Musicals and they will almost certainly bring their enthusiasm and favourite song from the movies and Musicals to their first lessons.

Understanding and developing sophisticated skills in Musical Theatre involves an appreciation of the **elements** that make up this extraordinary and universally popular art form. Using a traditional song as a starting point, this lesson explores the way in which a work of Musical Theatre is put together.

Teaching objectives

- To establish the elements of Musical Theatre
- To introduce students to ways of thinking about Musical Theatre.

Key facts, teacher's notes and in-class activities for students

Stage one: Introducing key ideas

Task 1

Here is an initial activity that helps to establish some vital foundations. Teach the following song –by ear and memory if at all possible – so that the entire class can sing it with confidence and without reference to the printed text or musical notes.

We believe this to be the original 'authentic' Folk Melody.

We would consider some form of drum pattern in the bass line. This could also be clapped by performers/singers.

First version

> Oh soldier, soldier, won't you marry me?
> With your musket, fife, and drum?
> Oh no, sweet maid, I cannot marry thee
> For I have no coat to put on
> Then up she went to her grandfather's chest
> And got him a coat of the very, very best
> She got him a coat of the very, very best
> And the soldier put it on
>
> Oh soldier, soldier, won't you marry me?
> With your musket, fife, and drum?
> Oh no, sweet maid, I cannot marry thee
> For I have no hat to put on
> Then up she went to her grandfather's chest
> And got him a hat of the very, very best
> She got him a hat of the very, very best
> And the soldier put it on
>
> Oh soldier, soldier, won't you marry me?
> With your musket, fife, and drum?
> Oh no, sweet maid, I cannot marry thee
> For I have no boots to put on
> Then up she went to her grandfather's chest
> And got him boots of the very, very best
> She got him a pair of the very, very best
> And the soldier put them on
>
> Oh soldier, soldier, won't you marry me?
> With your musket, fife, and drum?
> Oh no, sweet maid, I cannot marry thee

For I have no gloves to put on
Then up she went to her grandfather's chest
And got him gloves of the very, very best
She got him a pair of the very, very best
And the soldier put them on

Now soldier, soldier, won't you marry me?
With your musket, fife, and drum?
Oh no, sweet maid, I cannot marry thee
For I have a wife of my own.

OH SOLDIER, SOLDIER

2

Second version

For those of you who want a more complex situation. Feel free to add further garments and excuses.

Woman 'Oh Soldier, soldier, won't you marry me?
        With your musket, fife and drum?'

Soldier *'Oh, how can I marry such a pretty girl as you,*
        When I have no coat to put on,
        When I have no coat to put on?'

Narrator/chorus:

  So off to the tailor's she did go,
  As fast as she could run,
  And she bought him a coat of the very, very best,
  And the soldier put it on,
  And the soldier put it on.

Woman 'Oh Soldier, soldier, won't you marry me, now,
        With your musket, fife and drum?'

Soldier *'Oh, how can I marry such a pretty girl as you,*
        When I have no hat to put on,
        When I have no hat to put on?'

Narrator/chorus:

  So off to the hat-maker's she did go,
  As fast as she could run,
  And she bought him a hat of the very, very best,
  And the soldier put it on,
  And the soldier put it on.

Woman 'Oh Soldier, soldier, won't you marry me, now,
        With your musket, fife and drum?'

Soldier *'Oh, how can I marry such a pretty girl as you,*
        With a wife and two babies at home?'

OH, SOLDIER, SOLDIER

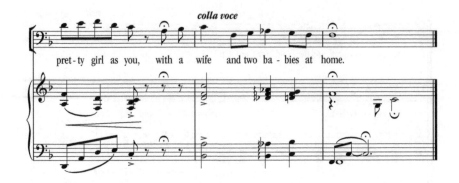

pret-ty girl as you,   with a   wife   and two ba - bies at home.

Task 2

Once the class is singing the song with flair and energy, pose them the following questions:

a) What do you think about the **context** of this song? When do you think it was written? What are muskets and fifes and what kind of drums do you imagine here? How do these details help date the song?

b) Who are the **characters** here and what appear to be their objectives and motives? What role does the chorus play and to whom are the various characters (including the chorus) singing?

c) What is the narrative arc of the song and how might this operate as a piece of Theatre?

Teacher's notes

Here is a real opportunity for you, as teachers, to discuss the role, importance and functions of a chorus and to explore the idea of sung dialogue.

Stage two: Deepening the understanding

Task 3

Now divide the class into groups of five and ask them

a) to discuss the various characters in the song, and

b) to devise a short musical play performance using the song. They must have total freedom to use the 'chorus' in any way they wish but must use the text and melody as written.

Task 4

Show and share the performances: each group must present their work in the same space in which they devised it and the 'audience' must gather round.

Teacher's notes
When the short presentations have concluded, the audience is encouraged to ask 'OK questions' (that is, questions that encourage positive attitudes and ideas about the decisions made by the 'performers').

Key facts
Now take a **closer** look at the material. The words of the song are the 'lyrics', so-called because in the Ancient Greek Theatre, which we believe integrated music, dance and drama, the words were sung to the accompaniment of the ancient stringed instrument known as the lyre. Similarly, the actions of those who make up the 'chorus' constitute the 'choreography'. What would constitute the 'book' of the short performance that has been devised?

Task 5

Creating the book: An extended activity
Using improvisation and discussion, challenge your students to devise a more extensive presentation, as follows:

a) Take five characters: the 'maid', the 'soldier' and three others who can be the 'chorus' and/or any other characters the students wish to create.

b) Create a story involving all these characters and improvise dialogue for them.

c) Decide which characters will meet, when and where.

d) The short scene must culminate in the singing of the song: it must arise naturally out of the action and must seem like sung dialogue.

e) Decide who the chorus is addressing and who they are themselves.

f) Show, share and discuss the presentations.

Teacher's notes
So 'the book' constitutes the play with its added elements of songs, lyrics and choreography. This is the unique blend that creates Musical Theatre. Now ensure that your students understand that the book and the lyrics may or may not be written by the same person and that there may have been examples of creatives who have also composed the music. What about the choreography? Does the performance of a show always need to have the same choreography? If not, how do you make your choice? Many of these topics will be explored further in future lessons but it is a good idea to sow the seeds early!

Topics for class discussion, student journal entries or essay assignments

1   Research who wrote the book, lyrics and music for five currently popular musicals and who devised the choreography. Ensure that students **always** credit these individuals when discussing any show or learning any song or dance routine. Find examples of shows in which book, lyrics and music are by the same person or any other combination of creative contributions.

2   Why is Musical Theatre such a popular art form?

3   What are the advantages of a form of Theatre in which all the dialogue is sung?

4   What are the problems caused by sung rather than spoken dialogue?

SAMPLE TEST QUESTIONS (MULTIPLE CHOICE)

1   The words of the songs in a Musical are known as: a) Verses b) Poems c) Lyrics d) Dialogue.

2   A 'fife' is: a) A kind of bagpipe b) A small trumpet c) A badge d) A small flute.

3   The storyline in a Musical is known as: a) The narrative b) The plot c) The development d) The tale.

4   The final line in the song 'O Soldier, Soldier' could be described as: a) The denouement b) The outcome c) The climax d) The result.

5   The 'chorus' in the song 'O Soldier': a) Comments on the action b) Narrates the action c) Takes part in the action d) Describes the scene.

6   One writer who sometimes wrote both lyrics and music is: a) Jerome Kern b) Stephen Sondheim c) Oscar Hammerstein II d) Leonard Bernstein.

7   The term 'choreography' originally implied the existence of: a) Several characters b) A tradition of dancing c) Elaborate costumes d) A chorus.

8   The term 'lyrics' came about because: a) The words were beautiful b) They were written to be accompanied by a lyre c) They involved honesty d) They were spoken fluently.

9   In any performance, acknowledgement should always be made to the writers of the music, the lyrics and: a) The storyline b) The book c) The review d) The vocal coach.

10 The song 'O Soldier, Soldier' is: a) A modern song b) A traditional song dating from the eighteenth or nineteenth century c) A song from a show d) A song from a Revue or the Music Hall.

Reflection: Lesson One

Students are invariably asked to reflect upon and analyse their learning experiences as they progress through school or College and it is important that teachers do the same.

Recently we observed a teacher working in a Performing Arts context who began a lesson by asking the students what they did 'last time'. Depressingly, it transpired that this question was not a means of stimulating the students to look back thoughtfully on their previous learning, but a genuine sign that the teacher could neither remember, nor had they kept a record of, the previous activities of the class! This situation is all too common with teachers who combine a busy performing life with teaching and, perhaps, work in several institutions.

We hope that Lesson One has demonstrated the need for careful planning and a sense of constructive purpose. It is equally vital for you to make notes of what you feel you have achieved and what remains to be done. This may well have been your first meeting with the class/group and you will have been at an early stage in building a professional relationship with them. The impressions you form of your students and their group dynamic will, of course, affect the way in which you use the following lessons but, before you think about the future, ask yourself the following questions:

1   What was the gender make-up of the class and how did this affect the success of the activities?

2   How did I ensure that all the students were engaged throughout the lesson and was I sensitive to the various approaches they demonstrated?

3   How did I encourage group work by spreading my attention around the various groups?

4   How did I ensure that the 'sharing' part of the activity was respectful and enjoyable?

5   How did the students' dress code or choice of dress reflect a serious approach to the work? How might I remedy this sensitively if I felt it was unsatisfactory?

Almost certainly you will have observed a wide range of confidence and ability in the students: some will be tentative in a subject area with which they are not totally familiar, whilst others will exude (probably false) confidence in what they hope will be an extension of their love of showbiz. That is precisely why we have introduced the work through a piece that is possibly unfamiliar and certainly not from a modern tradition. With that in mind:

1   How did the students react to the song you introduced and how might you help them to explore such material in greater depth at a future stage in their course?

2   What particular strengths did the students exhibit in the activity with the song?

3   How well did they respond to the multiple choice questions?

A short period of reflection following this lesson and the maintenance of a notebook or working journal will enable you to learn from the teaching experience and enrich the lessons that follow. We hope that this becomes a habit and a means of ensuring progressive mastery of each topic.

Lesson Two

Just Speak the Words! Acting in Musical Theatre

Lesson themes

Musical Theatre students will expect to enjoy singing songs from shows as part of their learning experience, but they should always consider **speaking** the text as a means towards singing a song effectively. This lesson outlines some ways in which students can begin to interrogate the text of the songs they are performing, creating the synergy between acting and singing that defines Musical Theatre.

Teaching objectives

- To enable students to explore the content, context and meaning of a song from Musical Theatre
- To establish ways of working that make this exploration possible
- To bring truth to performance

Key facts, teacher's notes and in-class activities for students

Stage one: Understanding and finding examples

Key facts

The Musical is a theatrical event which celebrates and encourages a collaboration between all the performing arts such as acting, dancing, singing, and significant aspects of spectacle depending on the subject material and style of the production. The 'musical' aspect of Theatre is identified in the use of song to heighten emotion, elaborate on the action of the piece, communicate mood and allow the thoughts to be carried by a melody that carefully illustrates the thoughts being expressed. This entices the listener to follow the narrative through song. The place of music within Musical Theatre can differ according to the style and purpose of the Musical.

Task 1

Set your students the task of investigating the ideas set out here:

Musical Theatre	Find and explore examples in the following genres of where the text pushes the music into action
Opera into Action	The narrative, text and music firmly intertwined in terms of the development of character and the use of keys to suggest relevant characteristics relating to the nature of the character singing, e.g. Mozart's *The Magic Flute*, where the Queen of the Night sings in a highly elaborated manner in order to identify her mystical and magical qualities; more 'popular' melodies for the two lovers Papageno and Papagena. This can also be recognized in works such as *The Phantom Of The Opera* by Andrew Lloyd Webber.
The Beggar's Opera by John Gay	Although referred to as an opera it was probably the first example of what we now understand as Musical Theatre; the text drove the music of the day into the narrative.
Vaudeville Post-1910s	The song will often be an 'isolated' thought not connected by narrative but rather part of a theme-based approach, e.g. love, historical or social conditions.
Revue Post-1920s	Often songs similar in style and often written by the same composer, such as Cole Porter or Stephen Sondheim. However, each song is not connected and might have already occurred in another Musical as part of a narrative.

Rodgers & Hammerstein Post-1950s	This partnership changed the relationship of the composer and lyricist and now the music score is conceived to create character and plot development, e.g. *South Pacific*, which identifies both 'love and social conditions'.
Spectacle and the Use of Technology Post-1980s	Musicals such as *Cats* and *Starlight Express* indicate that towards the culmination of the twentieth century we were moving away from the narrative and into a more experiential and spectacle-driven world of Musical Theatre. Gone are the 'two sets minimum' of the old-style revue to a change of setting for every moment of action possible, e.g. *The Phantom Of The Opera*, *Miss Saigon*, *Les Misérables*.

Key facts

From the middle of the twentieth century Rodgers and Hammerstein put their stamp on the development of Musical Theatre and the relationship between writer and composer. The lyrics and the music became interlinked and the familiar concept arose as to which came first, the chicken or the egg. We discuss their work again in Lesson Seven. In Musical Theatre, no matter whether the music came first or second, the music must be seen to have a place of importance within the narrative. The object of this lesson is to identify how actors and students can establish the qualities that music brings to the Musical and what we must do as performers to honour the stylistic and artistic decisions made for us.

In terms of music, a song may be repeated in different keys and sung by different characters within one Musical. This would not be possible in pure drama. Imagine repeating the speech of Jacques, 'All the world's a stage' at another point in the play just in case the audience didn't get it the first time? Do you remember the fuss when Hamlet's famous 'To be or not to be' speech was placed at the start of the National Theatre's production so that the audience would hear it fresh rather than miss it later in the play?

Stage two: Preparation

Task 2

Prepare five Musicals for your students to listen to, for instance: *Anything Goes*, *Oklahoma!*, *West Side Story*, *Cabaret* and *Evita*. Encourage them to either listen to a soundtrack or watch them on DVD. Then set your students the following questions or tasks:

1   What impact did the songs in each Musical have on you? How did you react?

2 Look at one musical number in each Musical and identify its importance to the plot and character development.

3 Can you identify any musical qualities that you enjoyed when studying these five Musicals?

4 Which song from which Musical had the most impact on you and why? Express reasons why the music/song gained such a reaction from you.

5 How important do you think the music score is within each of the Musicals? There is no need to be technical; just point out what you hear on your first hearing.

Task 3

From your students' knowledge of Musical Theatre repertoire, ask them to suggest:

1 Three singing popular artists who have sung material from Musical Theatre that they have 'made their own' and often sing in solo cabaret performances or 'Touring' performances. An example would be Barbara Streisand's singing of 'Don't Rain on my Parade'. Explain reasons for your choices and what decisions were made in the performance of the sung material.

2 Three songs from Musicals of your choosing that could not effectively be sung outside the context of the Musical's narrative. Explain reasons for your choices.

Stage three: Engaging with words

Teacher's notes

After many years of experience, we are still constantly surprised at the reaction of students to being asked to speak the words of a song. They will often:

1 Speak the words in the rhythm of the song.

2 Recite the words with little feeling or involvement.

3 Speak with little understanding of vocal variety, punctuation, phrasing and thought.

The fact that these responses are so common demonstrates how important it is for a performer to first be an actor engaging with the text before considering the musical structure and form of a song. In other words: it is not enough to sing your favourite number from a show in imitation of a well-known recording.

Task 4

Here are some ideas you might like to suggest to students as they read the text of a song:

- Speak the words as if you **want** to speak them
- Give the words a 'life' of their own
- Enjoy what you are saying so that you make the text meaningful to you
- Act out the words as if you are speaking them to someone
- Think about **why** you want to speak these words.

Teacher's notes

All these suggestions will elicit a variety of responses and, after a while, the message embedded in the text will be explored in some detail. The most important thing to remember at this early stage is that whatever the response to the task, **something** is being understood about the lyric being spoken and that is positive.

Once a song has been **sung** much of the necessary creative work has been shelved and so the **product** rather than the process has become uppermost in the performer's mind. By interrogating the text in detail before introducing the musical score, students should recognise the creative demands put upon them and will understand that exciting moment of transition when their personalized text becomes 'the song', created by another creative force: the composer/lyricist.

Assure students that, by being an 'actor' and speaking the text of a song, feeling the weight and structure of each word, they will bring that text to life. Because of the textual journey undertaken by a potential performer their unique contribution and creativity will come through in the final sung performance. By understanding the thoughts embedded in the text and then working with the musical score, the various conflicts and resolutions within the phrasing and melodic patterns will keep the work alive. An actor who creates character and an emotional journey by using only words to express the ideas and natural rhythms in spoken dialogue contrasts with the Musical Theatre actor/singer who works with the synergy of text and score to create a unique art form.

Task 5

Ask your students to carry out the following assignments:

1   Write out the lyric of a chosen song as continuous prose, deleting all capital letters and punctuation.
2   What do you notice about the words in this form?
3   In pairs, read the passage out loud: Fast, Very Slowly, Very Fast. Read it with very clear articulation and detail; whisper it both fast and slow. At this stage, avoid trying to make sense of the words.

4   Now speak the text through to yourself, marking with a (/) every time you feel the need to pause.

5   Discuss with your partner: why did you pause at the moments indicated? What were you thinking and why? Was it a habitual pause or were you out of breath? Discuss in pairs or groups.

6   Now speak the lines as if: talking to a friend in a café; talking with someone on the phone; whispering the thoughts to a pet dog; talking to yourself in the mirror; talking to a member of the family; talking to the character to whom the song may be addressed.

Stage four: Partnership between writer and composer

To appreciate the partnership between composer and lyricist it would be useful if your students could be given the opportunity to experience this artistic relationship. Here is a task that could engage your students with the role of lyricist with a composer.

Teacher's notes
Before starting, we encourage you to ask your students to have only a pencil, a rubber (try not to use it though) and unlined paper to hand when writing lyrics. Do not use computers and laptops. Everything must appear on the page as it comes into their minds. This will reflect so much of the process and no matter how untidy the page might appear, the way it is written on the page is the way that the ideas have been shaped.

The written page is the most flexible way of recording ideas and sometimes even arrows and circles or drawings will enhance the final ideas. Just let it happen and do not, whatever you do, try to conform to the verse form and regular metrical patterns until much later in the process.

Task 6

Ask your students to write a ten-line monologue on any theme or subject of their choosing. For this task we would suggest that they consider the following phrase: 'Why did I do that?'

Teacher's notes
When you repeat this exercise, we would suggest selecting different phrases and keeping them in a notebook for future sessions, so as to avoid repeating the exercise the exact same way.

Task 7

When they have completed writing the monologue, your students will need to rehearse the text, considering an identified setting. You might want to be flexible here but for a start we would suggest using a single chair as the stage prop.

Task 8

Enter the room with purpose (*think about where you have come from?*), see the chair and at an appropriate moment, whilst still speaking the text, sit down.

Teacher's notes
Do this two or three times. The reason for sitting down might change in each dramatic situation. It is important that the students always find their own reasons for entering the room and sitting. The actions must be seen to have an impact upon what they are speaking and thinking. This task will provide endless variations and opportunities to explore this stage of the process. The more they do this and share their ideas with you, the more they will learn about the process and why it is important to engage not only with the text but with the accompaniment. By the end of the speech they should be standing and just about to leave the room.

Task 9

Start by speaking the text sitting on the chair. Find a moment when you need to stand up and walk around the chair and make sure you are able to leave the room as you speak the final words of the text.

Teacher's notes
Often when a scene isn't working, this is a good tactic to employ just to see what happens. Remember that the solutions are identified in the action of speaking and moving the scene and in any discussion that you might have with your students. This is far preferable to giving the impression of always being in charge and having all the answers! Your students will enjoy this freedom in the teacher/student relationship. You will become partners in learning.

Task 10

Suggest to your students that they enter the room and see the chair, but for whatever reason they do not sit on it until they need to, when speaking the final few words of the scene.

Task 11

Ask the students to suggest the differences between the two scenes and which worked better for them, or where they found it difficult to make it work.

Teacher's notes

At this stage there might be a need for a slight rewrite of the scene. Students must realize that this reworking of the monologue is not a failure but part of the creative process between composer and lyricist! When completed, let your student/s identify which version they think is the most successful and identify the reasons why.

Task 12

Ask your students to perform the finalized scene.

Teacher's notes

While your students are performing the scene take note of any moments in the scene where there is a slight pause for whatever reason. When the scene is completed ask your students about why there were pauses. There will be many reasons for this, e.g. 'forgot the words'; 'out of breath'; 'didn't know what came next'; 'didn't have enough breath'; 'felt uncomfortable' etc. Talk about all of these moments and make your students aware that if there is a break either in thought or action in a monologue, the audience will often start to interrupt the flow of the dialogue and silently add in their own comments and thoughts about the scene.

The purpose of a monologue must be to drive the scene and to keep control of the situation. Having worked through the entire scene again and eradicated the unnecessary pauses there might still be a moment when your students want to communicate extra meaning. This is the opportunity for the monologue to open up into song. If this doesn't work, then a useful 'fall-back' is to suggest that the song comes at the opening of the scene or at the end of the scene. Identify whether the character wants to talk to the audience to give them information or whether they want to talk to themselves. Remember it really doesn't matter where the song comes in, so long as it has a purpose and holds the attention of the audience.

Topics for class discussion, student journal entries and essay assignment

1   Research the way in which various composers work/ed with their librettists or writers of lyrics.
2   How would you wish to work if you were a composer or librettist?
3   Why do you think that characters need to sing at certain points in a Musical?

4 What kinds of song can you identify? What, for instance, is a ballad or torch song?

5 How does acting in a Musical differ from acting in a straight play?

6 Is creating a character as relevant in *Chicago* as in *A Streetcar Named Desire*?

SAMPLE TEST QUESTIONS (MULTIPLE CHOICE)

1 The thoughts of a character in a Musical are conveyed through:
   a) Song b) Dance c) Acting d) A combination of all three.

2 Speaking the words of a song enables a performer to: a) Grasp the rhythm b) Dance expressively c) Explore the meaning d) Appreciate the rhyme-scheme.

3 The force that drives a character into action is known as:
   a) Motivation b) Ambition c) Purpose d) Sympathy.

4 When Rodgers collaborated with Hammerstein the lyrics often came:
   a) Last b) First c) At the same time d) After a long struggle.

5 A Musical demands: a) A synergy of text and score b) Memorable tunes d) Lively dance numbers d) Good jokes.

6 Acting in a Musical demands: a) Ambition b) Star quality c) An ability to use the words with understanding d) Good ballet technique.

7 Exploring the words of songs from a Musical is an essential part of:
   a) Singing in tune b) Preparation c) Memorizing songs d) Energy.

8 When performing a number from a Musical you should: a) Base your singing on that of a popular singer b) Work towards your own unique interpretation c) Exploit your dancing ability d) Relax.

9 In a Musical the music: a) Drives the action b) Provides a background c) Introduces popular songs d) Creates atmosphere.

10 The concept of a 'triple threat' performer is: a) A historic idea b) A relatively modern idea c) Unrealistic d) Outmoded.

Reflection: Lesson Two

Some years ago we were invited to assess a young performer singing 'On the Street Where You Live' from the Musical *My Fair Lady*. The song begins with the words 'I have often walked down this street before'. After he had finished singing, we asked the singer: 'Where do you imagine you are when you sing this song?' To our amazement he replied 'on stage'. This simple moment illustrates some of the issues that may well have emerged as you worked in this lesson. Clearly, our student, like us, had failed to differentiate between 'you': the performer, and 'you': the character. It is, of course, the character whose inner life and experience we should be exploring and that process involves a very careful mode of thinking which your students may have found difficult or surprising in this lesson.

If you think back over your experience with the method and material we have suggested, allow your mind to wander over that song 'On the Street Where You Live'. What do the words tell us about the origins of the song? The simple use of the preposition 'on' as opposed to 'in' for example, tells us that the lyrics are written by an American librettist: in the USA people tend to say 'I live on this street' whereas, in the UK they would say 'in this street'; indeed, in the UK it would be more frequent to use the word 'road' rather than 'street'. That small detail is not simply fascinating and informative; it also reveals the level of attention which you are trying to instill in your students. As you reflect on this lesson, therefore, you should be planning to demand a much higher level of attention to the words than you or your students may have been accustomed to.

The levels of success which students achieved with the various acting/ speaking exercises we have suggested in this lesson may well have varied considerably: why was this? To what extent was this due to a) previous lack of experience, b) reluctance to broaden horizons or take risks, and c) failure to understand the underlying purpose of the activities?

As you think about this, do be reassured that all such experiences with this kind of material are perfectly common and that students are frequently demonstrating levels of insecurity as they work. Try, now, to reduce the experiences encountered to a few simple principles which sum up the key learning points you wanted to make and begin to plan how you will address them in future. For example, we have discovered that whenever a character or several characters in a Musical sing a song (however well-known), the performers ought to be able to give accurate and in-depth answers to the questions 'Who are you?', 'Where are you?' and 'What is happening to you?'

Had our student from our opening story in this Reflection asked these questions of himself, his answers would have been very different!

Lesson Three

'Playing the Dots'

Lesson themes

Most of us associate Musical Theatre with memorable tunes and expect to leave a performance singing them either aloud or in our minds! The fusion of words and music is a key element for students to explore and it may well depend on the support of some form of accompaniment. Understanding how words and music work together and how best to use either live or recorded accompaniment are essential elements of education in Musical Theatre and require both imagination and sensitivity on the part of teachers, accompanists and students.

Teaching objectives

- To provide insights into the relationships between the main elements of Musical Theatre
- To focus on the role of music in Musical Theatre
- To extend students' knowledge of the repertoire of Musical Theatre
- To give guidance on the use of accompaniment
- To help students in interpretation of song and its relationship to acting.

Key facts, teacher's notes and in-class activities for students

Stage one: Introducing the topic

Key facts

Audiences in a theatre expect to share the 'inner lives' of the characters they are watching and hearing. However, in order that the characters become credible human beings they will need to exhibit recognizable behaviour traits and speak or sing accessible language. The performer is required to differentiate between addressing the audience directly or enable the audience access to their private thoughts.

Task 1

Encourage your students to identify the difference between speaking to yourself and speaking to the audience.

Teacher's notes

Points to consider will include: how the speaking to 'self' or 'others' (audience/ unseen characters) impacts upon the vocal and physical delivery of the character at that moment. Establish the volume/energy, mood and objective for the thought spoken. Might the character be frightened, determined, happy or concerned?

Task 2

Prepare a set of simple popular song melodies that you can recommend to your students, or preferably, encourage them to choose one for themselves.

Task 3

Set your students the task of writing a short poem, to be referred to as a 'lyric' from now on, based around these intimate 'thoughts' at this moment in the monologue.

Teacher's notes

Now aim to encourage your students to use the given melody to find a way that allows the 'lyric' (thoughts/words) to fit in with the melody already existing in the song chosen for this purpose. In reworking the text to fit in with the melody of the proposed song, your students will engage intimately with the skills required of the librettist. These will include: how to fit the words in, make them rhyme (if needed), have a complete thought within each phrase and many other factors that might arise by doing this work. This will take time and there will probably be several outcomes before students agree on the final result. This is a positive outcome as it gives you much to talk about and develop in relation to understanding the music of the song. When the final version is agreed students will identify: the skills of how to fit words to music, phrasing, relevant volume and where the main impact of the thought is communicated through the melody of the song chosen. This will now become the students' personal song lyric.

Task 4

Experiment and perform the piece using both spoken and sung voice to express the entire scene.

Teacher's notes

Engage your students in reflecting upon the success of their scene and repeat the performance to see if they can discover any further points regarding the performance of the monologue scene. When this has been completed a few times and the work is secure, aim to play or get someone to play the music accompaniment to their piece or find a backing track that can be used. Perform the scene again making sure that answers to the following questions are secure in the performance process.

1   Did you have to change the words around to fit your thoughts or the music?
2   Did any phrases change and if so for what reason?
3   How did the melody impact upon the thoughts sung?

Explore the total performance experience and identify what you observed when working with the intimate text and setting it to the music of a familiar 'pop' tune.

Key facts

Students need to understand that:

Now, in effect, they have been at the coal-face of creating a piece of Musical Theatre. They have deepened their understanding of being a librettist by using the musical material suggested. By working through this process they have already discovered facts about this work that couldn't be put into a textbook. There is nothing like the experience of doing to provide understanding and clarity.

Having completed the monologue task, it would be worth repeating the exercise from 'scratch'. The repetition of the task is the important learning opportunity and should never be considered boring. Students are boring if they groan at being asked to repeat a task! Find the joy in this work and they will benefit enormously. Repetition and rehearsal are the life blood of this art form.

By repeating this exercise and creating lyrics to a well-known popular song, students will refine the process and begin to understand what skills are required to write music for lyrics. As a result, their artistry will improve and their understanding of what is required of them in performance will become greater. They will also develop respect for the stylistic decisions undertaken before a singer begins to work with the sung material.

Stage two: Exploring words and music

Key facts

In Musical Theatre there is a belief that the character work should always begin with the text driving the thoughts. Others will encourage you to believe that the music drives the action. This argument is ongoing and has often had disastrous impacts upon artistic collaborations, such as that between Brecht and Weill. A disagreement as to what came first was the main reason for their splitting up and going their separate ways in the mid-1930s. Sondheim's *Merrily We Roll Along* and *Curtains* by Kander & Ebb both explore the dilemmas between the lyricist and composer and yet, despite this, they are the essential ingredients that enable Musical Theatre to exist.

Task 5

Set the students the task of researching as many partnerships within the genre of Musical Theatre as they can. Find out who did what and listen to their music and write comments regarding the qualities of songwriting and the style created by each partnership.

Stage three: Understanding the accompaniment

Key facts

Any performer in Musical Theatre relies on a musical accompaniment for their work, whether it be to support a melody, create tension and juxtaposition or complement what they are singing. They may be provided with a pause in which the accompaniment replaces their singing for a while or there may be indications of dance or movement embedded in the music.

At one time, any performer in Musical Theatre relied on a pianist who could invariably sight-read from sheet music and support the singer in auditions or in learning a song. If you are fortunate enough to have access to such an accompanist it is vital that they are integrated into your plans and activities and not relegated to a role in which they are simply expected to play 'on demand' without any other involvement in the preparation or concept of the work. The worst possible scenario is when a pianist resorts to playing louder to support inadequate singing! More often these days students and teachers have come to rely on pre-recorded accompaniments and are thus deprived of the live, creative interaction between two or more musicians. The essential quality to develop in students is an ability to use and respond to an accompaniment rather than allow it to simply enable them to sing the right notes.

Teacher's notes

If you can play the piano, that's great; if you have limited or no keyboard skills, the following task might be very useful in supporting the work of your students in this aspect of your teaching.

Take any classical piece of music with a good melodic line which is often singled out by a solo instrument. Find a section that feels complete and is not too long in duration. Romantic composers such as Rachmaninov, Tchaikovsky, Schumann, Brahms, Offenbach and Puccini tend to have good melodies. Look at adverts for ideas. They tend to use Romantic music to help their marketing sales.

Task 6

Considering versions, A and B endeavour to get your students to (i) listen to the different piano accompaniments; (ii) record both accompaniments; (iii) improvise a simple melody using both accompaniments; and (iv) add a lyric to your improvised melody.

Here is an example of a simple harmonic sequence that most students learn to play on the keyboard.

VERSION A: 4 bars in 'C'

Here is an upbeat version of the same harmonic sequence in a different key that you might like to use with your students. Encourage your piano students to improvise and have fun with this.

VERSION B:

Here is the same accompaniment with an added extended melody that most piano students will recognise from 'jamming' on the piano. Now encourage your students to create their own melodies and add words to create a song in a musical theatre style.

Here is another simple chord sequence played over the tonic pedal note C. Let your students experiment with these set of chords until they find a pattern they like. Look at the melody with simple text.

WAS HE PUSHED?

Gently ♩ = 110

All the King's men tried for hou - rs, glu - ing Hump - ty's bits in place,

mp

All the King's men al - so thought why was an egg sat on a wall, how

sil - - ly is that tale_____ can it be true,_____ and did he

2

fall?_____ Or was he pushed? I guess we'll ne - ver know   the

truth._____   truth._____

The simple chord sequence used in this version is as follows:
1 – C (bass) (C-E-G); **V** – C (bass) (G-B-D); **IV** – C (bass) (F-A-C); **V** – C (bass) (G-B-D);
Remember: Always return to opening chord when you want to finish your 'own version' of the song **1** – C (bass) (C-E-G).

When your students have mastered the above chord sequence why not get them to invent their own melody or create a different lyric to suit the work being created. Perhaps your students could make the lyric relevant to their specific situation. See what happens.

Hey presto! Your students now have the ingredients to create a musical theatre piece of their own. Bravo!

Teacher's notes

Don't worry about the subject material for the time being. Consider any subject from the mundane to the exotic. These might include a news item, a comment on a newspaper article or even the weather forecast. By doing this exercise students will come across a variety of issues and problems which can be discussed at each stage of the process. It is important that they must be prepared to perform their own versions.

The question you should always ask your students: Why write something for someone else to sing that you are not able to speak or sing yourself?

Here is a possible idea for a Musical Theatre number based upon the famous chord sequence of Pachelbel's Canon

WHO HID THE COFFEE?

This is yet another way of creating a musical theatre number by using a well-known chord sequence.

Task 7

When they have completed Task 6, give your students a 'standard' from the *American Song Book* and ask them to perform the song lyric to the rest of the group.

Topics for class discussion, student journal entries or essay assignments

Thinking about any song you have encountered in your work, respond to the following questions:

1 How would the singer phrase each thought – short or long phrase? What kinds of impact do these create on the listener?

2 Do you feel the style of the writing reflects the quality of the text?

3 Are there any clues in the music? Do phrases repeat themselves, and why?

4 Are the rhythms complicated or simple?

5 Does each phrase start on the first beat of the bar or is each expression on the back foot?

6 Look at the intervals used in the music. Are they melodies by step or angular and difficult to sing?

7 How do the dynamics, phrasing, rhythms, time signatures and tempi affect the potential performance of the song?

8 Having explored the text fully, do you think that the music changes with the various thoughts of the character? If so, how?

9 How are repeated phrases dealt with in the music? Are there similar melodic phrases or different ones, and why?

10 What happens to the character throughout the music?

11 How long is the introduction? What is happening to the character before they sing?

12 What are the gaps in the vocal line creating for the character and the audience?

SAMPLE TEST QUESTIONS
(MULTIPLE CHOICE)

1 The accompaniment to a song is: a) An optional addition b) An integral part of the music c) A decoration for added effect d) A support for the singer.

2 The argument as to whether the music or the words drive the action in Musical Theatre has: a) Sometimes caused rifts between creative partners b) Never been entirely resolved c) Resulted in constant discussion d) All three of these.

3 Repetition is essential in preparing for a Musical Theatre performance because: a) It is boring b) It helps the memory c) It refines understanding d) It keeps the director happy.

4 The meaning of the words of a song often depends on: a) Tempo b) Phrasing c) Volume d) Pace.

5 The emotional impact of a song may be created through: a) Volume b) Timing c) Changes in pace d) Key changes.

6 A good accompanist will: a) Help the singer to sing the right notes b) Provide a complement to the singer's performance c) Determine the speed of the performance d) Determine the volume of the performance.

7 If there is a live accompaniment to a song the overall pace must be decided by: a) The singer b) The pianist c) A discussion between the singer and accompanist d) Listening to a recording.

8 The blend of instruments chosen by the composer to accompany a song is known as: a) The score b) The orchestration c) The band d) A riff.

9 A song in which two singers take part is known as: a) A duo b) A duet c) A partnership d) A dialogue.

10 A change in energy in a song is often achieved through: 1. Greater volume 2. A change in rhythm 3. Vibrato 4. Slowing down.

Reflection: Lesson Three

The completion of this lesson is a good opportunity to reflect on the progress you have made in establishing that singing a song or passage from a Musical is a form of acting. This approach may have come as a surprise to your students, but you should not allow that to divert you from keeping that concept as a foundation of your work. A great deal will depend on your own background: you may have primarily trained as a musician or dancer, or you may have been working with colleagues for whom the world of acting seems remote and threatening: whatever your situation, think now of the demands you have made of the students and how you can reassure them as they explore an integrated art form.

This lesson highlighted the role of accompaniment: how did you introduce this important topic? If you and your students relied entirely upon pre-recorded accompaniment, how did this affect the originality of any performance? If we think of singing in this context as a form of acting, how would your students react to the great Polish director who told his cast that their performance must be 'born afresh in them each night'?

The human relationship between accompanist and singer provides rich potential for individuality, subtle changes and slight variations, so how might you compensate for this not being available and what opportunities does your situation allow for providing students with this experience?

If you are fortunate enough to have good keyboard skills or you have access to colleagues who are fine accompanists, it is worth reflecting on how you can develop your students' ability to relate creatively and courteously to that provision. Sometimes the attitude that singers demonstrate towards their accompanist can verge on the dismissive: what did you do in this lesson to ensure that this is not the case with your students?

Sometimes, the teaching of a song is left to a teacher sitting at a piano: what aspects of the work in this lesson ensured that working on a song is much more than achieving musical accuracy? Is the entire teaching team and approach working in harmony?

At this point in your teaching, it is helpful to compile notes showing what you have observed in the voices and physicality of each student. These are relatively early days and there may be remedial work to be done: notice how students move and breathe and think back over how each individual reacted to the tasks you set. Your future planning will depend on these observations as well as on a range of topics and levels of understanding that you will want to introduce.

The range of abilities in your students will now have become more obvious and you may have to consider making changes to groups or finding ways to support those who are obviously less confident or comfortable. Did you, in this lesson, convey the impression that you were observing everyone in the class or did you find yourself focusing on the few? In our experience, one of the most frequent complaints amongst Performing Arts students is that of perceived favouritism. Did you avoid giving this impression?

Lesson Four

'I Could Have Danced All Night!'

Lesson themes

For many years, enthusiasts of Musical Theatre claimed that it was the choreographer Agnes de Mille working with Rodgers and Hammerstein on their Musical *Oklahoma!* (1943) who first integrated dance into the Musical Comedy in such a way that it became an equal partner with the music and acting. That view has been challenged by some scholars, but the fact remains that dance has now become fundamental to Musical Theatre rather than remaining a decorative afterthought. Indeed, some Musicals now take much of their life from various dance forms: think of the jazz-ballet opening of *West Side Story* or the tap dance opening of *A Chorus Line*.

Teaching objectives

- To establish connections between the ideas of 'the chorus' and 'choreography'
- To investigate where dance is appropriate and what purpose it serves in a Musical
- To investigate some of the major dance styles used in Musicals
- To explore the experience of learning dance numbers.

Key facts, teacher's notes and in-class activities for students

Stage one: Understanding the role of choreography

The dance and movement in a Musical are potentially the most exciting and inventive of the variables that make up the work. Whereas the text and the score are more or less fixed, the choreography can be created afresh for every production. Far too often teachers feel that they must slavishly reproduce a version of the 'original' choreography they have seen in the theatre or via recorded media, but this is not always necessary and can have a deadening effect on the new interpretation of the work. When we turn to explore new and original Musicals in a later lesson we shall draw upon the insights hopefully gained from this lesson.

Teacher's notes

As a teacher you are likely to encounter a wide range of dance ability among your students: some will have attended dance classes from a very early age and others may simply enjoy moving to the rhythms of songs without any particular dance vocabulary. It may not be realistic to expect your students to develop into 'triple threat' performers with equal skill in singing, dancing and acting unless they are aiming to make Musical Theatre their career. At the same time, you may have limited dance skills yourself and feel the need to import a professional choreographer if you are directing a show.

Even with such limitations and varied experiences it is perfectly possible to educate your students in vital aspects of dance for Musical Theatre and you may well find that you have students in your group who can provide personal experience from which others can benefit. We have found that the dynamic of a group can often be enhanced by having some experienced dancers among the students who are usually pleased to take a lead when needed.

Key facts

The great problem with dance in Musical Theatre is that it is often taught by rote rather than arising out of an understanding of the needs of the characters, the context and the communication of ideas which are part of any drama. Accordingly, we shall be suggesting ways of thinking about dance that may well begin with research, questions and observation.

The contemporary Theatre invariably expects Musicals to use dance as an important ingredient which may well determine the whole tone and style of a production. Not only does the term 'choreography' derive from the Greek concept of a 'chorus': a group of performers who comment on the action of the main characters; it now also may provide the very foundation on which the show is built. For example, the musical adaptation by Andrew Lloyd Webber of T. S. Eliot's poems into the Musical *Cats* depends for its success on the choreography of the entire cast by Gillian Lynne.

Task 1

Now that many Musicals are known through both stage and screen versions, the opportunities for watching and learning are almost limitless. We suggest that you have your students watch and focus on dance sequences in some of the following: *Cats, Chicago, Oklahoma!, West Side Story, A Little Night Music, Show Boat, Les Misérables, Hair, The Phantom Of The Opera, Hamilton.* Who were the choreographers, what was unique about their work and what purpose did dance serve in these shows?

Stage two: Experiment

Task 2

In groups of five or six, take any one song from any one of these shows and devise a short dance sequence that seems to catch the mood of the song. The moves can be as simple as you wish.

1 Decide what it is you are trying to communicate through the dance, then show and share with the rest of the class.

2 In response to any feedback from the teacher and rest of the class, work on moving from total stillness to action and back again, concentrating on the ideas of 'focus' and interpretation of the mood and content of the song. At this stage, the 'dance' must be much more than a set of learned steps, however simple the movements involved.

Teacher's notes

Of course, we all want our students to move/dance well and, where necessary, master a sequence of movements that contribute to the drama. But, in the same way that their singing and acting must be much more than learned notes and words (however accurate), so the dancing must be much more than, for example, a mastery of some unusual steps originally created by Bob Fosse!

Task 3

Now ask your students to study the following list drawn up by the choreographer Margot Sunderland in her book *Choreographing the Stage Musical*:

The role of choreography in a Musical

1 To generate energy.

2 To express moods and heighten feeling states.

3 To complement other media.

4 To change atmosphere.

5 To add humour.

6 To entertain.

7 To add spectacle.

8 To display costume.

9 To further relationships.

10 To enhance characterisation.

11 To convey physical states.

12 To display ritual and celebration.

13 To manipulate time (accelerate, slow, suspend).

14 To heighten suspense.

15 To evoke phantasy, dreams or the unconscious.

16 To further the plot.

Then, either with reference to the piece just devised by the groups or after watching a filmed/video version of a piece of choreography from a show, decide which were relevant to that 'performance' and how they influenced the artistic decisions made.

Task 4

Now introduce some of the following examples of dances which form an integral part of various Musicals and either watch or work on at least two such dance numbers according to the size and ability of your group of students:

Cabaret: dances in a night club

My Fair Lady: the ball scene

Grease: the dance contest

A Chorus Line or *Easter Parade*: the demands of a chorus dancer

Saturday Night Fever: a disco contest

West Side Story: either the opening dance or 'America'

All that Jazz: the demands on a Broadway Dancer.

Stage three: Understanding roles and relationships

Key facts

Students and teachers need to understand the importance of a clearly thought-out and sensitive relationship between such 'creatives' as the director, musical director and choreographer of a production. Whereas the director must retain an overall concept and vision, this must be based on a complete understanding of how the musical director wishes to interpret the score and how, in turn, the choreographer hopes to interpret the rhythmic and melodic aspects of the music in dance routines. All three creatives must agree on the dramatic function of the music and dancing. The choreographer may have to make a contribution after the musical and dramatic landscape of a Musical has been established, but that does not mean that the choreographer is meekly compliant. All creatives need to have a deep appreciation of the choreography as part of their total concept of the work. Discussions and disputes must take place before rehearsals begin and this invariably demands careful preparation.

Teacher's notes

There is nothing more frustrating than a musical director or choreographer drifting into a rehearsal with a few vague ideas about what they would like to try out while the cast of performers are hoping for clarity. There is always room for the 'let's try this' approach but any task must be related to a clear concept of the desired impact of a sung/danced number.

Task 5

Divide your class into groups of three and ask each student to adopt one of the following roles: director, choreographer, or musical director, so that there is one of each in every group. Now ask each group to select a Musical and listen to/watch a recorded performance of a short extract. Each student, in role, then describes their concept from what they have seen/heard. Share the results.

Stage four: Dance and movement

Key facts

There is a great deal more to choreography in a Musical than teaching and learning dance steps, whatever the style. Dance and all forms of physical movement need to be an integral part of a performance, not an extra added on to a song or chorus activity. Choreography needs to embrace every aspect of physical performance, ranging from the movements of individuals acting through song to entire casts singing and dancing in an elaborate 'number'.

Whatever decisions are made about movement they need to be made in the light of understanding the **cultural context** of the Musical. This is a concept we shall encounter again in Lesson Seven.

Here are some fundamental questions that will help in establishing this essential idea that will, in turn, determine how performers will move in any one Musical:

1   Where and when is the action set? Were there any 'dance crazes' at the time?
2   What clothes and fashions are the characters wearing? Don't forget footwear.
3   What ethnic/racial cultures are evident?
4   What styles and forms of music are used in the show? These might include jazz, heavy rock, soul, classical, orchestral or disco.
5   Are any dance styles specified: e.g. waltz, hip-hop, street dance, tap?
6   Is dance a part of the culture of the characters: if so, what forms does it take?
7   What beliefs and attitudes are evident in the storyline?
8   How free or restricted is the human body in the context of this work?
9   What real/imagined age are the characters?

Now take a closer look at the nature of the music and ask:

1   Are there forms of music that take their names from dance? For instance waltz, jive, serenade, tango, hip-hop or rock 'n' roll?
2   How is the music distributed in the show? Are there, for example, opening and closing choruses or actions interspersed with songs and duets?
3   What moods are evident in the music?
4   If characters sing, who are they singing to?
5   Are characters required to sing and dance simultaneously and, if so, how expansive/energetic does the dance need to be?

Now consider the choices made that might affect any attempts to teach movement and dance to the cast:

1   Where is this to be staged?
2   How large a cast can fit on the stage?
3   What will the audience see?
4   What is the floor surface like?
5   What will the 'dancers' be wearing? Do you have a say in this?

6 How will you teach/learn the dances/movements with music? Will there be recorded music or a live accompaniment for rehearsals?

7 How important or relevant is it for you to use the original choreography?

Teacher's notes

In his remarkable autobiography *Tainted by Experience* (2000) John Drummond, who once directed the Edinburgh Festival and a major radio network, tells how he had a meeting with a number of 'creatives':

> Not one of them mentioned the audience. They talked about everything else, but whether or not an audience existed seemed not to matter to them at all.
>
> 359

As a teacher you will constantly need to point out that the audience is 'reading' a performance and that this is particularly the case with how they see and interpret dance and movement.

Stage five: The language of dance and movement

Task 6

Get your students to form a circle, thus creating a space which they are asked to enter from time to time: this is 'on stage' if you prefer to use that terminology. Ask them to slowly enter and then leave the space as you point to chosen individuals and explain that they must show by the way they enter and leave one of the following emotions:

a) Uncertainty that they are in the right place.

b) Confidence that they are in command of the space.

c) A desire not to be noticed.

d) A sense of awe or wonder at what they find.

e) Panic and wish to escape as soon as possible.

f) Total relaxation as if they have arrived at a place they have always longed to be.

Now play some dance music and repeat the process with students entering and leaving the space in the same mood, but in time with the music: they can spontaneously create improvised dance steps or simply move to the rhythm of the music. Finally, after several experiments with your students, ask them:

What is the movement or dance in all these situations **trying to say?**

This is the central question for all dance and movement in a Musical and it may, at this point, be a good strategy to ask students to watch some more examples of dance from Musicals and ask themselves that same question.

Teacher's notes

Remember that the most potent movements emerge from stillness and it is important to work with students to develop the ways in which they can move from relaxation, into focus and then into movement.

Task 7

Working with the entire group (using music if you wish) help your students to acquire basic choreographic vocabulary by introducing them to:

a) **Canon:** a term taken from music in which a single movement or sequence of movements by one dancer is repeated by one or more other dancers. This can happen after the first dancer has completed the movement or during it. If the latter is the case it is called a 'ripple canon' and can give the impression of gathering energy.

b) **Concertina effect:** this is something to avoid! It occurs when the spacing in an equidistant group is lost in travel. Now work on having the group move around with specified distance between them that must be maintained!

c) **Dosy-Do:** this term derives from folk dance but can still be used to great effect. Partners face each other, walk towards each other and pass back to back (either passing right or left shoulders) and finally walk backwards towards their original starting places. This is an enjoyable exercise if you gradually increase the speed of the movements without losing the precision.

d) **Equidistant grouping:** try getting your students to form a group shape in which they are all equally spaced and can form a tidy group or several groups. This is known as 'formation' and will feature in many 'chorus' Musicals.

e) **Freeze:** use the same group shape as in the previous exercise and have them move for a count of three and then remain entirely still for a count of three before moving again. Experiment with the nature of the movement and incorporate **gesture:** a movement of a limb which makes no contact with the floor and is therefore different from a **step**.

f) **Isolation:** ask students to make a movement in which one body part is out of its usual position. This might, for example, be the shoulder, head or knee. By *isolating* this part from the rest of the dancer's body it draws attention to it and will give the movement of the rest of the body a very distinctive character. See what happens when everyone chooses to isolate the same body part.

g) **Level:** experiment with the height at which movements take place: e.g. low level in a normal standing position or high level with heels off the floor and standing on tip toe. What is the effect of varying levels?

h) **Pas de Bourree:** this is a frequently used running step, usually comprising three steps (left, right, left or right, left, right) but performed over two beats in time. The steps, for example, might be: behind, side, front or front, side, behind (r,l,r or l,r,l).

i) **Peripheral movement:** where limbs are outstretched and the movement are performed away from the body centre. Experiment with movements in **unison** and then in **canon**.

j) **Syncopation:** this musical term is often employed in dance movements. The stress patterns of an expected rhythm are disturbed so beats are either missed or unaccented beats will be accented. Music with a strongly accented bass line/sound will be helpful for this exercise.

k) **Tempo:** another opportunity to point out the relationship between dance and music. Explore performing simple movement sequences at different speeds. What is the effect?

l) **Transition:** this comprises a movement or set of movements that act as a bridge between two different dances, themes or phrases or may be a link between singing, dialogue and another dance event. Think of the work you did on 'Soldier, Soldier' in Lesson One. How might you link two 'events' by movement/dance?

Stage six: Shall we dance?

Key facts

Preparation for the performance of a Musical should always begin with a careful reading of the text and musical score. A total grasp of the storyline and the setting of the work is an essential tool for every member of the creative team. It is not always obvious from this initial study whether or not certain songs or musical numbers should be 'danced' and it is important to justify the dancing of any 'number' before the preparatory phase goes on any longer. It is possible to 'over-dance' a Musical and obscure the plot altogether but this, obviously, does not apply if the entire story is built on dance. Sharing the time imaginatively between dialogue, song, music and dance is an essential ingredient of successful Musical Theatre. If we remember those qualities that dance can bring to a production (see Task 3) and study the content and position in the show of each musical number carefully we can determine the contribution that dance can make. For example, after a reflective ballad and a section of dialogue there may be a loss of energy that can be remedied by dance.

Traditionally 'opening numbers' of Musicals are strongly sung and danced and that process may well be repeated in subsequent Acts to remind audiences of the mood of earlier action or establish new directions. But there are remarkable exceptions. For example, the opening of *Oklahoma!* is notable for having cheated the expectations of its original audience by its lack of glamorous 'chorus girls' in its opening moments. Dance can equally take the form of a 'production number' where the stage is full, the music powerful and the action at its height. Such moments might need to be juxtaposed with moments of humour or a danced response to the gentle flowing qualities of contrasting music.

Patter songs or rap make particular demands on movement: nothing must detract from the brilliance and complex structure of the text and yet the performer cannot be static. Physical replication of the rhythmic patterns of the sung words is not enough: this is an area for exciting experiment and imaginative choreography.

Teacher's notes

In teaching Musical Theatre you may not be required to choreograph a production but the principles and ideas we are setting out in this section should enable you to deal creatively with introducing an extract or single song from a Musical. Some of the ideas may seem simplistic and assume very little previous knowledge or competence on the part of your students, but it has been our experience that students of very mixed abilities may have access to programmes of study. One University we taught at included students with visual impairment and considerable restrictions in movement and hearing.

Key facts

The perfect marriage of music, poetry, dialogue and dancing is not a new concept; indeed, it was a required attainment of educated people in Renaissance Europe and Britain. In the modern Musical we have rediscovered this idea after a period in the early days of this form of entertainment when dance was merely a decorative addition.

Task 8

Ask your students to read the following descriptions by a professional dancer of three currently popular Musicals, paying particular attention to what is said about the dance content.

Hamilton: tells the story of the forgotten American Founding Father, Alexander Hamilton, and his ascent out of poverty against the backdrop of the American War of Independence. Hamilton was white but born in the West Indies. Dance is integral to the plot and styles include a mash-up of jazz and hip-hop to swing and jitterbug. The music tells the story through rap, elements of jazz, British pop and classic Broadway. It references a variety of creative artists from Rodgers and Hammerstein to The Notorious B.I.G. The result is a pastiche in every sense. The cast are predominantly African-American and Hispanic.

Six: is a modern retelling of the lives of Henry VIII's six wives, presented as a modern pop concert. Each wife takes it in turn to tell her story and we are left to decide which one of them suffered the most. The winner will become the group's lead singer. Like the eclectic score, the choreography draws from a variety of genres: jazz, house, hip-hop and commercial modern dance.

The Book of Mormon: was an immediate success on the West End stage when it transferred to the Prince of Wales Theatre after a record-breaking Tony Award-winning opening in New York in 2012. Written by the creators of the cartoon series *South Park*, this Musical Comedy is frivolous, naughty and downright shocking – no taboo left unturned and lots of bad language. The dance styles used are mixed genres from modern theatre dance to African. The plot revolves around two missionaries who are sent from Salt Lake City to preach in a remote Ugandan village. It is a satirical examination of 'The Church of Jesus Christ of Latter-Day Saints' and its beliefs and practices.

Now ask your students to break into groups and select a song from any one of these Musicals. Let them devise an almost spontaneous, improvised dance sequence, using any of the dance styles listed above. The emphasis should be on spontaneous reaction to the music but should then challenge the students to find ways of moving their 'choreography' around a space or find ways of dancing for an imaginary audience.

Stage seven: Teaching choreography

If you are a teacher with dance skills you will certainly be called upon to devise and teach dance routines for Musicals and provide students with the experience of preparing the dance aspect of a Musical Theatre production. You may well also be asked to give advice and guidance to performers on any aspect of physical movement, perhaps during a solo song or duet. Keeping in mind all that we have explored in this lesson, here are some key points to remember:

1 Ensure that your students/performers begin from a position of relaxation and readiness.

2 Be careful to take deep, controlled breathing into account in any movement you devise/demand.

3 Remember that your dancers may well be singing at the same time as dancing: what does this mean?

4 When selecting a dance style in conversation with other creatives, remember that a term like 'hip-hop' covers a wide field of cultural references that may include music, dance, fashion, art, writing and recording.

5   Ensure that students move effortlessly from one mode of performance into another: for example, if they move from a relatively static song into a dance routine in an instrumental interlude, work to make the transition as natural as possible. Think, for instance, of the relaxed and apparently effortless way in which characters in the movie *La La Land* moved from dialogue into dance.

6   Avoid imposing clichéd gestures onto a song: for example, shading the eyes to represent 'looking into the distance' or clutching the heart for emotion. By all means encourage illustrative gesture if it adds significantly to the communication, but it must arise naturally from the context and serve more as a form of 'visual punctuation' than an end in itself.

7   Take care of your voice and use it with restraint. Far too many teachers play very loud music and bellow at their students in the hope that this will inspire them to learn. The result is militaristic rather than artistic!

8   There is a dance tradition that the best dancers tend to move to the front of the 'class' and that they expect 'corrections'. This has little place in the world of teaching and creates a negative and unpleasantly competitive atmosphere. As a teacher you should show equal concern for and attention to an entire group and praise what is well done rather than concentrate on what is wrong.

Topics for class discussion, student journal entries and essay assignments

a) Who have been some of the most successful choreographers in the world of Musical Theatre?

b) How important is it to preserve and reproduce the original choreography in subsequent productions of a Musical?

c) Are there Musicals where the choreography seems to be part of the original writing?

d) Why are the opening sequences of *West Side Story* so important in dance terms?

e) How influential has the Film Musical been in shaping the way we see dance in Musicals?

f) Watch the movie version of *Oklahoma!* and look for the moments when the dancers are clearly not singing (The voices are dubbed). How has the concept of the 'triple threat' emerged and what are the problems of trying to attain this status?

SAMPLE TEST QUESTIONS
(MULTIPLE CHOICE)

1 The successful choreography of Gillian Lyne established the popularity of: a) *West Side Story* b) *Cabaret* c) *Cats* d) *A Chorus Line*.

2 A bridge between two sections of a dance or action is called: a) An interlude b) A flow c) A transition d) A link.

3 The following Musicals were memorable partly because of the choreography of Bob Fosse: a) *Sweet Charity* b) *West Side Story* c) *Chicago* d) *The Phantom Of The Opera*.

4 The term 'choreography' derives from the Theatre of: a) France b) Africa c) Ancient Greece d) Italy.

5 The essential aspect of music for dancers is: a) Melody b) Tune c) Rhythm d) Pace.

6 A Musical that tells of the wives of King Henry VIII is: a) *Six* b) *Show Boat* c) *The History Boys* d) *Camelot*.

7 A Musical that tells aspects of the lives of its dancers is: a) *A Chorus Line* b) *Oliver* c) *Sweet Charity* d) *42nd Street*.

8 The aim of any choreographer must be: a) To make the dancing distinctive b) To integrate with the music and acting c) To reflect the music d) To be the most distinctive element of the show.

9 A choreographer must always keep in mind: a) That the performers have to breathe b) That the performers are wearing specific costumes d) That they must drive the dancers to get the best results d) That they are working with sensitive people.

10 Dance in a Musical must be: a) Obtrusive b) A contribution to the storyline c) An element in itself d) Distinctive.

Reflection: Lesson Four

This lesson, perhaps more than any other so far, will have provided an opportunity for you to see the divergent and varied abilities of your group of students. Dance tends to be a highly specialized subject, although like singing, almost everybody does it in some form!

Did you observe that, in dance activities, the more experienced dancers moved to the front of the class? That tends to be a tradition and you may feel that it is inappropriate in this context. As you watched the class responding to a variety of stimuli you will have noticed those who were almost dancing before they began, such is the way in which rhythm infects their body. Others will have been far less confident and you should keep a careful note of those for whom the introduction of dance is a threat to their confidence. You will have noted their answers to the questions on the concept of the 'triple threat' and from this point onwards you should be asking yourself 'what is a reasonable expectation for a Musical Theatre student?'

When you invited the students to create even the simplest of steps and sequences, were you aware of those who brought particular ethnic traditions of dance to their work? If such traditions were not evident is there a way in which you might encourage this in the future?

As you reflect on the experience of this lesson you might ask yourself the following questions:

1   How did the students cope with the combination of singing and dancing, especially with reference to breathing?

2   What is the physical position in the teaching space/studio from which it is best to teach a dance sequence?

3   Is it preferable to face or have your back to a group of dancers when you teach some choreography?

4   Do I need the help of a professional dance teacher/choreographer for future projects and, if so, how do I organize that?

5   What is the most suitable form of musical accompaniment to employ as I attempt to integrate dance, singing and acting and how can I achieve that?

You will probably have noticed that the introduction of movement and dance into your class greatly increased the energy levels of the students. This is something to exploit and develop. Perhaps each future lesson might include a 'warm-up' based on the activities you introduced. Make a note of the students who could be useful choreographers for the future: other students invariably respect those who have advanced dance skills. The obverse of this is that your future lessons must be as rewarding and challenging for the expert dancers as for those who act or sing with greater skill.

Working towards developing a performer who combines both ability and imagination in all three areas will remain one of your main objectives. Integration in the Arts has always been a fascinating yet contentious topic and has engaged the thinking of some of the pioneers of modern Theatre practice: some reflective reading around this topic at this point will enrich your experience. (see Sources and Resources. p.153–4).

Lesson Five

Where Did It All Start?

Lesson themes

You may well ask why there is any value in tracing the origins of Musical Theatre with modern students! The answers are:

1 Some of the earliest works still contain some of the best and most memorable moments and 'numbers'.
2 An understanding of the origins of Musical Theatre will provide essential insights into the ingredients and problems of that art form.
3 The necessary research will provide an invaluable model for future practice.

Teaching objectives

- To provide an overview of the origins of Musical Theatre in the West
- To extend an understanding of the nature of this art form
- To encourage individual research.

Key facts, teacher's notes and in-class activities for students

Stage one: Discovering theatre history

Teacher's notes

You do not have to think of yourself as a Theatre historian or researcher in order to inspire your students to explore the origins of Musical Theatre with you. The precise moment in which Musical Theatre as we know it today came into being is, in itself, a fascinating debate and there are no easy answers.

Key facts

Gerry Tebbut (2000) makes it seem very simple when he tells of a production of a melodrama called *The Black Crook* at Biblo's Garden Theatre in New York in 1866, to which were added songs, dances and lavish scenery because a troupe of French dancers were working at a nearby theatre when it burned down and were in need of a home! 'The show' says Tebbut, 'was a riotous success and ran for 474 performances in New York and for many years on tour. The Musical was born!'

Such statements certainly provide pointers from which we can begin our searches but, in your reading, you will come across various facts that may well seem to contradict such definite suggestions. The secret is to look at as many sources as you can and ask your students to do the same. For example, the volume dealing with American Drama in the excellent *Revels History of Drama in English* (1977) gives very fascinating details of *The Archers* by William Dunlap, a show which clearly combined spectacle, song and romance, which was performed in 1796 and had some of the characteristics of what came to be known as 'Musical Comedy' and, eventually, 'the Musical'.

Teacher's notes

If you encourage your students to research these early years of Theatre on both sides of the Atlantic they will find numerous examples of the combinations of scenic spectacle, dance, music and drama which were described by an almost bewildering variety of names. For example, between 1790 and 1820 we come across such terms as 'historical comic opera', 'melodramatic romance', 'musical drama' or 'grand pantomime ballet'. When it comes to **discussion** with your students these provide rich material.

Stage two: Exploring sheet music

Key facts

A further very important fact emerges as we look at early productions that have some of the characteristics of the Musical, and that is the role of **sheet music** in the process of making works popular with members of the public who may not have been able to see or hear the original production. Long before the era of mechanical recording, music from successful shows was published in a form that enabled people to play the pieces on their pianos and sing the songs in their parlours. For example, 1855, once again at Biblo's Garden Theatre in New York, saw the first performances of *Rip Van Winkle*, an 'opera' with music by George Bristow and libretto by J. H. Wainwright.

This production by an English management is generally regarded as being the first American opera. It proved very popular with audiences but its popularity was greatly increased by the publication of a 'parlour edition' of some of the most well-loved songs as sung by their 'star' Louisa Pine.

Task 1

Students often have difficulties in relating to earlier periods of history or to events outside their experience. We have provided an obvious example of how this can be remedied by the mention of early sheet music. Much of this material is still available and can be used and experienced. Even fifty or sixty years ago the sheet music of popular songs was being published alongside recordings, so get your students looking in charity and second-hand bookstores for examples. If you have students who can play the keyboard/ piano here is a chance to build some interesting work around their skill and if you can obtain full scores of Musicals or operas from a library then help your students familiarize themselves with what these look like.

Task 2

If they have difficulties relating to earlier periods such as the nineteenth century, challenge them to name buildings that they see daily that might date from that period or invite them to research a talk about their family history and what songs their great-grandparents might have sung. Our experience is that history can seem much nearer than it first appears if you make it personal.

Stage three: Finding the true origins

Key facts

The real origins of what has become Musical Theatre are far more distant than the eighteenth or nineteenth centuries.

Teacher's notes

Students should be encouraged to undertake their own investigations, but it would be helpful to provide an outline. We have already seen with the song 'Soldier, Soldier' that it is possible to build a drama where the words (dialogue) are sung rather than spoken and this has been the case in many cultures for many centuries. It was certainly employed in the early years of the Christian Church and probably in other religions.

Musical Theatre as we have come to know it evolved out of the art form we call 'Opera', which emerged from a group called 'The Camerata' in the Italian city of Florence during the late sixteenth century. This is a topic well worth researching but the essential facts are that this group was concerned with a revival of Greek Drama and was anxious to understand the role of the 'chorus' in production. They began to experiment with dramas in which the dialogue was sung and the subject matter was taken from Ancient Greek Myths, of which the story of 'Orpheus and Euridice' was a particular favourite.

Teacher's notes

It is important for teachers and their students not to be intimidated by the concept of **opera**. It is no longer the preserve of a monied elite or indeed, of great metropolitan opera houses. Live relays or excellent recordings of productions are now widely available and there are many small-scale touring opera companies throughout Europe and the English-speaking world who bring fresh, accessible works of Musical Theatre of all kinds to local venues. New generations of gifted young artists have emerged to bring life to historic forms of entertainment: the field has never been so rich and suitable for study.

Key facts

The early attempts in Italy to create 'music dramas' were somewhat pedestrian, but fortunately a composer of genius – Claudio Monteverdi (1567–1643) – began to write for the genre and produced some superb works.

Early operas were performed at court but, with the growing popularity of this type of music-drama, it was necessary to build Opera Houses, which enabled elaborate staging and spectacular effects to be included in the performances. Rich costumes, dancing, beautiful scenery and clever stage effects have remained important aspects of all forms of music drama to this day. Later in the seventeenth century the writing of opera spread to England, where the composer Henry Purcell (1659–95) produced some of the most beautiful theatre music of all time. His settings for plays by Shakespeare (re-written by the poet John Dryden) are still worth exploring.

As the seventeenth century progressed, opera gradually emerged from the simple telling of a story to become an elaborate display of virtuoso performance skills by famous singers. In this process the careful integration of acting, singing and dancing, which was the intention of the original pioneers of opera, became lost in the petty rivalry of performers and impresarios.

In the London of 1710 and for the next thirty-five years, Italian Opera, or 'opera seria' as it was then known, was almost the preserve of the German composer George Frederick Handel (1685–1759) and the music of his operas remains a legacy for all young singers today.

It was obvious to the composer Christoph Gluck (1714–87) that opera needed reforming and returning to its roots with an emphasis on pure representation of character. His works and ideas helped to rescue opera from being merely a musical entertainment. Gluck's opera *Orfeo* (1762) remains one of the gems of Musical Theatre.

Opera seria concentrated on mythological and classical stories and invariably consisted of a small cast, sung speech (recitative), elaborate arias and sometimes a 'chorus' consisting of the main characters singing together. Even in England the performances were in Italian. A progression was clearly needed!

Stage three: Practical exploration

Task 3

Divide the class into groups of six. Challenge them to listen to the story of Orpheus and Euridice:

Orpheus was the son of one of the muses (who inspired the arts) and was the greatest singer and musician in Ancient Greece. The god Apollo had given him a lute and he could charm almost anyone with his music. He married the nymph Euridice and was devastated when she was bitten by a snake and died. He journeyed to the underworld to rescue her and he charmed the god of the underworld, Pluto, to allow Euridice to return to life with him. However, Pluto and his partner Persephone insisted that Orpheus should not look at Euridice during her return to the world, but he could not resist turning to look at her and so lost her forever.

Ask your students to devise their own version of this drama with music. It could be like a radio play, podcast or soundtrack, or it could be fully acted out with your choice of songs and other music. It might help you to know that a British TV version entitled *Orpheus on the Underground* (metro) was very successful. Set the drama in any time and location you wish.

Stage four: Opera and Musical Theatre progress

Key facts

By the time that the Austrian composer Wolfgang Amadeus Mozart (1756–91) came to write for the great opera houses of Vienna and Salzburg, he was creating works with multiple human characters: noble and common men and women, servants, sons and daughters all engaging in sung or spoken dialogue and frequently singing elaborate conversations or engaging in elaborate physical and naturalistic business. This new style came to be known in Italian as 'Opera Bufa' or, more commonly, by the French term 'Opéra Bouffe', and was widely imitated throughout the opera houses of Europe and, eventually, America. Characters sang in their own language, and in England John Gay wrote his 'Beggar's Opera' using not only his native language but traditional music drawn from folk songs and ballads.

Opera in Italy continued to exert a huge influence on the nature of Musical Theatre. Composers like Donizetti (1797–1848), Rossini (1792–1868), Verdi (1813–1901) and Puccini (1858–1924) wrote operas of expansive proportions in which the chorus became an important protagonist, the settings were often contemporary, the action was underscored by atmospheric music and arias and recitative were fused into profound psychological dialogue. The plots were often taken from Romantic novels, real historical events or the plays of Shakespeare and the acting/ singing demands were of ever-increasing physical and emotional difficulty. For example, Donizetti's opera *Lucia di Lammermoor* (1835), based on a novel by Sir Walter Scott, contains a scene in which the leading performer has to sustain fifteen minutes of solo singing in a scene of madness and distraction.

Teacher's notes

The central point for you, as a teacher, to emphasize is that it is these demanding Italian operas, along with those of the German composer, Richard Wagner (1813–83) that continue to provide the bulk of the repertoire of the world's opera houses. It is the vocal discipline and technique required to appear in such works that continues to shape the way in which singers are educated at the highest levels.

The links between what is sometimes rather loosely called 'grand opera' and the modern Musical Theatre that your students are exploring may not always be obvious, but they are, in fact, profound and fascinating. For example, the term 'rock opera' is meaningless, if you do not know what 'opera' entails!

Before we consider some aspects of *Opéra Bouffe*, which flourished in Paris and spread its influence to Vienna, London and New York, it is important to emphasize that as teachers we are not engaged here in archaeology or the life of a museum. The works we have described are **living works of art and are always best explored through the medium of performance**. Video recordings and live relays from major theatres and opera houses are widely available and even if you can only introduce one aria, chorus or duet for your students to listen to, you will widen their horizons to an unexpected extent. It is often good practice to have your students download a range of versions of a single aria/song and let them decide which they prefer and why.

It is also important both for you and your students not to become obsessed with **definitions**: in this subject area they can be quite slippery and you may find considerable differences between various sources. We shall encounter that problem in our next section.

Stage five: Orpheus again

Teacher's notes

Introducing your students to Offenbach's *Orphée aux Enfers* (Orpheus in the Underworld), which was first performed in Paris in 1858, is a demonstration of how you can help them to make connections in their growing understanding of the development of Musical Theatre. They will probably know the tune of the famous 'gallop' (usually now thought of as a Can Can) but not much else.

Key facts

Orphée is a good example of the way in which France enabled the *Opéra Bouffe* to develop in very distinctive ways, which were later to export to both Great Britain and America. In retrospect we can see here the emergence of many of the characteristics we now associate with modern Musical Theatre.

With a libretto by Hector Cremieux and Ludovic Halevy and music by Jacques Offenbach, the show was first performed at the Theatre des Bouffes-Parisien in Paris and subsequently in Germany (1859), Austria (1860), the USA (1861) and Great Britain (1865). A new version of *Orpheus in the Underworld* opened on Broadway in 1883.

The original Parisien audience would have been aware of and have venerated Gluck's *Orfeo*: there was, and still is, a substantial tradition of classical learning in France and a considerable opera scene. However, Offenbach's version of the story was a **parody** of the serious opera with spectacular dancing and a far from tragic end for the main characters. These elements of humour, colour, happy resolutions to the problems in the plot and memorable scenic effects might have initially shocked an audience, but Paris had gradually been developing this new form of entertainment, which sometimes earned the name of *Opéra Comique*. This name does not necessarily imply 'comical' but rather like our term 'comedy', a non-tragic end to the story and a variety of art forms on display.

Orphée aux Envers was by no means the first such production to be seen in Paris. Since 1848, an actor, singer, playwright, musician, composer, conductor and Theatre producer who called himself just Hervé had already begun to devise various types of *Opéras Bouffes* that included original music, singing, dancing, spectacular scenery, amusing or historical storylines, jokes, beautiful costumes, witty dialogue and fast-moving action. Such shows became a very popular alternative to the more serious kinds of opera and formed the basis of what came to be known as *operetta* and *comic opera*.

Stage six: English language theatre

Teacher's notes

It is unlikely that any of your students will have encountered forms of theatrical censorship or restrictions on what may or may not be publicly performed. Hopefully, they never will have this experience. However, by the time Hervé was making his experiments with new performance modes in Paris, most of the major cities of England had strict legal limitations on what was permitted to be performed in theatres. This had a profound effect on the kind of productions that were possible.

Key facts

From 1737 the 'Licensing Act' placed two restrictions on what was allowed in public theatres: firstly, **only** the two theatres with royal patents – London's

Covent Garden and Drury Lane – were permitted to produce 'legitimate drama'; secondly, **all plays** for public performance had to be submitted to the Lord Chamberlain for a license.

We shall encounter these issues again in Lesson 11, but students will probably recognize the continuing importance of the Theatre Royal, Drury Lane and the Royal Opera House in Covent Garden in the continuing world of Musical Theatre. The effect on all the many other theatres in England during the years following the Licensing Act was to provoke a whole range of experiments in finding ways to get around the law! These included creating a show from a variety of loosely connected items (we still use the term 'Variety'), underscoring the action of classic plays with music, turning the dialogue into rhyming couplets, having the dialogue sung, using lavish spectacle, introducing provocatively dressed chorus girls and making drama out of legends and fairy stories. Such performances were variously described as 'burlettas', 'burlesques' or 'extravaganzas' and became the vogue even after aspects of the Licensing Act were abolished in 1843. The origins of what we now call 'the Musical' and, in the UK, 'pantomime' are obvious and make a rich field for student research.

Stage seven: Into performance

Task 4

Ask your students to devise a short (max ten minutes) version of a play by Shakespeare in which they find ways **NOT** to present it as a straight play.

Task 5

Advise students to investigate the life and career of J. R. Planché. How did he introduce ideas from the French Theatre to the UK?

Task 6

Give your students the following challenge: create a very short version of a well-known fairy story and involve singing, dancing, dialogue and, if possible, lavish costume. Perform this to your fellow students and invite them to react vociferously! Is your work a 'burletta'?

Task 7

Learning a song from early music drama.

Ask your students to think about this:

Every November in a London Street named 'White Hall', a solemn drama is enacted on a Sunday known as 'Remembrance Sunday'. This ceremony involves leading members of the Royal Family and Government and includes a large Military Band as well as many current and former members of the armed forces. The major actors in this national drama gather around a simple stone memorial called the Cenotaph and lay wreaths in remembrance of those who have lost their lives in war. The entire event is witnessed or heard live and on broadcasts by an audience of millions and the climax for many is the total silence of two minutes ended by a bugle call.

However, for many observers an even more dramatic moment during this ceremony is created a little earlier when, as the main participants gather, the Military Band of Guards, dressed in sombre grey, play the lament 'When I am Laid in Earth'. The sinking bass line and haunting melody of this piece seem to fill the entire space of the gathering and bring everything to a state of collective grief and reflection.

This description of the event at the Cenotaph is permeated with terminology from the Theatre but this seems entirely appropriate: there is a stage and an audience, there are actors dressed in special costumes using a specific script and carrying out deeply symbolic actions and there is carefully selected and timed music. In fact, it could be argued that this act of Theatre is built around music.

Appropriately, the music of 'When I am Laid in Earth' is taken from another piece of Theatre: Purcell's opera *Dido and Aeneas* (1689) in which a lovesick queen laments her desertion by a lover before taking her own life. The original music was scored for performance in a theatre by a small ensemble of stringed instruments and a solo voice but, in order to create the 'Remembrance' event, it has been re-arranged for an outdoor performance by a large Military Band.

Now find recordings of this piece and, if possible, after careful listening, try singing it yourself and staging the moment when Dido sings it. Compare various versions of performance and decide which captures the essence of the number for you.

Topics for class discussion, student journal entries and essay assignments

Teacher's notes

Students will need to understand that the development of Opera was an aspect of the 'Renaissance' and that this movement is something they must investigate.

a) What is the precise meaning of 'Renaissance' and where and when did it take place?

b) Why did early composers/creators of Opera draw on classical mythology for their storylines?

c) How does an opera with 'recitatives' and 'arias' differ from a Musical or Musical Comedy?

d) How many operas based on the myth of Orpheus and Euridice can you discover? Why do you think that this was such a popular choice of subject matter?

e) As elements of the Theatre Licensing Act were relaxed in the UK, other theatres were permitted to present 'legitimate drama'. Such theatres became known as 'Theatres Royal'. Does your hometown have, or did it have, a Theatre Royal? If it did, find out about its origins.

f) Why do you think that the word 'pantomime' has acquired such different meanings in France, the United States and the UK?

g) What kind of regimes usually impose theatrical censorship and why do you think it emerged in eighteenth century England?

SAMPLE TEST QUESTIONS (MULTIPLE CHOICE)

1) The plots of early operas were usually drawn from: a) Legends b) Works of literature c) Classical mythology d) History.

2) 'Recitative' is: a) Spoken recitation b). Sung dialogue c) Intoned speech d) A Melody.

3) Opera as we know it today had its origins in: a) Italy b) France c) Great Britain d) The United States.

4) Opera which told the stories of common people came to be known as: a) Opera Seria b) Burletta c) Opera Bouffe d) Comic Opera.

5) The first 'Musical' is sometimes said to be *The Black Crook*, which was produced in New York in: a) 1820 b) 1900 c) 1866 d) 1956.

6) The popularity of some early Theatre works which included music was enhanced by: a) Street singers b) The publishing of sheet music c) Famous conductors d) The invention of the phonograph.

7) The word 'Pantomime' in Britain describes: a) Acting without speaking b) A short opera c) A lavish entertainment based on a fairy story d) Clowning.

8) Plays began to resemble modern Musical Theatre with the addition of: a) Casts of children b) Singing and dancing c) Electric stage lighting d) Live animals.

9) A nineteenth-century production that included lavish spectacle and a great deal of music and dance might have been described as: a) A light comedy b) An extravaganza c) An operetta d) A classic.

10) Audiences gradually grew tired of burlesques and the form that replaced them was the forerunner of what we now call 'The Musical'. It was known as: a) Light Opera b) Musical Comedy c) Satire d) Opera Bouffe.

Reflection: Lesson Five

Engaging Musical Theatre students with history may be a giant leap for some of them: what was your experience and how might you build on the knowledge and understanding you aimed to provide and encourage?

In our experience students are generally ignorant of Opera and aspects of Theatre History but, given an imaginative introduction to the topics, will rapidly become fascinated and amazed. Fortunately, it is no longer necessary to visit an Opera House in order to watch a spectacular performance: leading companies now arrange live streamings from their theatres and there has been a rapid development in the growth of small-scale touring opera companies. If you can follow up the lesson you have just taught with exposure to a live performance you will have the opportunity to reinforce the learning achieved, especially if you provide some pointers as to what your students might observe.

How did your students' reaction to the topics introduced in this lesson relate to the understanding you aimed to develop in Lesson One? Did they recognize the elements of Musical Theatre that might be common in the Musical or the Opera?

By introducing the idea of music from one context being used in another ('Dido's Lament', for example) you can encourage your students to recognize many kinds of music-making as a form of Theatre. When you next work with the class discuss how a rock group, jazz ensemble, famous singer or even a symphony orchestra might use the elements of Theatre to make their performances attractive to audiences. If you do this, the historical aspect of our subject will seem far less remote. Students should be able to appreciate the same features of Theatre in any given period.

One of the topics you have introduced is the idea of sung dialogue. This element of Theatre will recur frequently during this course of study and it demands careful thought. On the surface it is an absurd activity and it is important to reflect on why it is so effective and popular. Why do we accept the convention that characters talk to each other in song or think aloud to a musical accompaniment? How do we move from spoken dialogue into sung dialogue and why do we accept this as normal behaviour when we go the theatre?

These questions must underpin your work and activities. Exploring the conventions of theatrical performance with your students might have begun with this lesson on the emergence of Opera.

How many current performers or directors can you name who have 'crossed over' between plays, operas and Musicals? Increasingly there is mutual respect between art forms and, following this lesson, you might wish to consider how you can contribute to and encourage this welcome aspect of our work. Even though the course is focusing on Musical Theatre, it is vital to remain open to multiple influences from the world of the arts and, particularly, you might now reflect on how or if your students made connections with works from the past.

Lesson Six

'Pogroms in the East' – Europe Comes to the USA

Lesson themes

In 1977 Walter J. Meserve wrote 'Musical comedy must be considered one of American Theatre's major contributions to world theatre.' How did this come about? If you look at the names of many of the most famous creators of Musical Theatre you will notice that many of them suggest a Jewish-European origin. Take, for example, Oscar Hammerstein, Leonard Bernstein, Lorenz Hart and Stephen Sondheim. But were these the only immigrant communities to make a contribution to American Musical Theatre?

Teaching objectives

- To investigate the immigrant origins of Musical Theatre in New York
- To establish important facts about the life and works of major writers and composers
- To encourage creative thinking about the origins of Musical Theatre and its links with 'classical' and 'black' music.

Key facts, teacher's notes and in-class activities for students

Stage one: Identifying the subject area

Task 1

Before you go any further, make sure your students know who the key figures we have mentioned in the lesson themes are and what they are famous for.

Task 2

Ask your students to discuss these questions: Why these obviously Jewish names? How many other writers of Musical Theatre have Jewish/European origins?

Stage two: Understanding a 'different world'

Teacher's notes

Modern students may have little or no concept of theatrical conditions in earlier periods of history: they are so familiar with the contemporary digital age and the ever-changing means of recording and creating performance that the world of nineteenth-century Theatre is a complete mystery to them. But this is a world they need to understand in order to study Musical Theatre. When we speak of musicians these days – instrumentalists, conductors or composers – we probably think of them as working in concert halls, clubs, venues or recording studios but in the nineteenth century they would invariably have been working in theatres.

Key facts

Towards the end of the nineteenth century and in the early years of the twentieth century, the opera houses and theatres of Britain, mainland Europe and Russia all had substantial resident orchestras. All forms of theatre music were performed live and there was no facility for recorded music. Accordingly, theatres also had their own resident composers and conductors, who were responsible for providing music, often original, for all productions.

Many of the musicians – players, conductors and composers – were Jewish. This, however, was a period of great prejudice and antisemitism and many Jewish people were subjected to hate and intimidation. Unsurprisingly, modern students tend to think of the horrors of Nazi Germany as an example of hatred of Jewish people, but in fact antisemitism was a problem long before that. For example, the great advocate of Naturalism in literature and Theatre, Emile Zola, was opposing widespread anti-Jewish sentiments in the Paris of the 1890s. Similarly, there was considerable prejudice against Jews in the old cities of the Austro-Hungarian Empire such as Vienna, Prague and Budapest, all of which had opera houses and concert halls in which Jewish musicians were prominent. The prejudice often resulted in violence and discrimination.

These 'pogroms' (i.e. acts of violence towards a particular ethnic group) meant that a substantial number of Jewish people, including many musicians, fled the violence and emigrated to the United States of America, where by 1880 there were already some five thousand theatres or opera houses. Indeed, New York became the centre of a large Jewish community and the impact on the emerging theatres and opera houses was very considerable. Today, some eight million Americans trace their origins to Germanic/Jewish families.

Not only did Jewish musicians make a substantial contribution to the Theatre, but they also used their talents in the growing film industry and ensured that the totally unnecessary distinction between what has been termed 'classical' and 'popular' music did not inhibit the growth of new and exciting kinds of Musical Theatre.

Teacher's notes

It might be preferable to refer to so called 'classical' music as 'orchestral' music, as this gives a far more accurate description of what we hear in the theatre or movies: **what do you think?** When it comes to singing we sometimes describe artists as 'classically trained' when their repertoire is taken from the work of composers who wrote music heard mainly in the concert hall or recital room, but there are now many singers and other musicians who see themselves as 'crossover' artists, drawing on what we might think of as jazz, rock and orchestral and recital music.

Stage three: Widening horizons

At this stage you might point out that:

- Jerome Kern, who composed the music for what many consider to be the first, great American Musical *Show Boat*, had studied classical composition in the German city of Heidelberg before his family was forced to flee to the United States
- Leonard Bernstein (who was born 100 years ago) has been celebrated as a composer who enabled performers to engage with many genres within the Theatre because of the breadth of his compositional styles.

Teacher's notes

Here is an excellent opportunity to consider some of Bernstein's work in some detail, but this might take some time. You may prefer to set the following tasks:

Task 3

Discover and discuss what other ethnic groups of immigrants to the US have influenced the kinds of music and performance that we now call 'Musical Theatre'?

Task 4

Think about and listen to recordings of the song 'Summertime', which comes from the opera/Musical *Porgy and Bess* by the Jewish/American composer George Gershwin. Amazingly, this song has already had 25,000 'covers' in styles ranging from jazz and gospel to rock and rhythm and blues. Its varied influences have been remarkable: for example, in 1956 Mahalia Jackson's recording became an anthem for the Black Civil Rights movement and two years later it was popularized through the 'biopic' *Rhapsody in Blue*. By 1969 Janis Joplin's version had become a symbol of the 'hippie' movement and Ella Fitzgerald's later recording was established as a classic of jazz singing. Even though the composer, Gershwin, was Jewish, the storyline of his Musical deals with the lives of another deeply oppressed race: African-Americans.

Teacher's notes

Exploring with your students the various versions of this song taken from a work for the stage will enable you to remind them of its original context and how a song can embrace emotional states and strong individual ideas. The words are like a soliloquy in a drama where a character shares their inner life with the listeners.

It is highly likely that your students will include those of both African and Jewish heritage, and it is essential to consider these legacies with equal attention and energy. Contemporary teachers and their students have no excuses for ignorance of the shameful legacy of slavery, which brought so many millions of individuals from West Africa to the 'New World'. Dutch, Portuguese, French and British colonialists were trading with slaves from the 1400s but the date of the arrival of the first African slaves in the Americas is usually given as 1619. There are now abundant websites and some Museums of Slavery which chart the story of slavery up to and beyond its abolition in the USA in 1865.

Key facts

Incredibly, an older generation of teachers may remember such Variety Theatre productions and TV programmes as *The Black and White Minstrel Show*, in which white performers 'blacked up' to simulate groups of negro musicians. This incredibly insensitive act would fortunately now be deemed unacceptable, but it did contain some clues as to the vital contribution of black culture to music in general and Theatre in particular. Jazz, soul, hip-hop, rap, blues and scatting are only some of the features of black music that have shaped our Musical Theatre.

Ironically, African slaves, arriving after terrible conditions at sea, were forced to share in Christian worship, and they became aware of biblical narratives of the oppression of the people of Israel and their hope of a 'promised land' in Palestine, together with hymns that celebrated Bible stories and expressed a longing for a 'promised land' of life beyond the grave. Combining their sufferings with a legacy of vibrant and complex drumming and dance rhythms and haunting natural vocal harmonies from African culture, the enslaved people began to devise their own 'hymns'. Expressing their longing for freedom, they sang *Deep river . . . my home is over Jordan . . . deep river, Lord, I want to cross over into camp ground*' and other such evocative songs which came to be known as 'Negro Spirituals'. From such music both blues and 'gospel' emerged.

The origins of black music in Theatre are also rooted in the work and life of slaves. At some stage, enslaved Africans developed the habit of sitting in circles singing and accompanying themselves on improvised percussion instruments such as bones, drums and one-stringed fiddles. Although slaves would have arrived speaking a variety of languages, they eventually evolved a dialect of English which was often unkindly parodied. From these ingredients African-Americans created a form of entertainment involving witty dialogue between characters who came to be known as 'Interlocutor' and 'Bones'. The precise origins of the Minstrel Show are a matter of some conjecture but the idea of making the elements we have described into a form of Theatre was exploited by a white performer who 'blacked' himself: Thomas Dartmouth Rice. Rice claimed to have learned a song and dance routine by observing an elderly African stableman; he bought the man's clothes and added his own songs to those he heard and embarked on a successful career as a showman. Ronald Harwood (1984) tells us that between 1840 and 1880, Rice's show became 'the most popular form of entertainment in the United States' and that 'his appearance at the Surrey Theatre, London in 1836' launched the enthusiasm for Minstrel Shows in both Theatre and on television, which persisted well into the 1970s.

Teacher's notes

The condescension towards black people represented by the kinds of entertainment we have been discussing is a topic for debate with your students, but we can see here considerable influences on the development of American song and dance and, through the integration of dialogue, song, dancing and storytelling, we can see the evolution of such forms as vaudeville, music hall and revue.

The moment would come when the Theatre would enable African-Americans to tell their story through opera, Musical Comedy and the Musical.

Stage four: Applying knowledge

Task 5

Divide the class into groups of four students then ask them to:

Imagine that you and other members of your group are immigrants who have come to the United States to escape persecution, poverty or both. These are some of the emotions you might experience:

- Homesickness
- Relief and Hope
- Fear of the unknown
- Determination to preserve beliefs and customs
- A sense of comfort in hearing familiar music.

Can you find songs from Musicals that capture some of these emotions? Now weave one or more of these into a short, improvised scene in which an immigrant arrives in the USA.

Stage five: A detailed case study

Key facts

We have already mentioned the librettist Oscar Hammerstein, who is usually known as Oscar Hammerstein II. In lesson 3 we pointed out that, after writing for a number of other composers, he collaborated with Richard Rodgers to create the most successful Musical Theatre partnership of all time.

BUT:

Who was Oscar Hammerstein I? He was not the father but the **grandfather** of Oscar Hammerstein II and his story is typical of how influences from Europe infiltrated the Musical scene in New York. Hammerstein actually 'ran away to sea' as a boy from his native town of Szetin, which is now in Poland. He went first to Liverpool in England and then sailed to the USA. His flair for innovation and business eventually turned him into a leading Theatre impresario, opening opera houses and ensuring the development of Musical Theatre in the New World. He wrote musical plays and staged major productions by other writers.

Hammerstein's grandson, Oscar was to become one of the giants of Musical Theatre: widely recognized as one of the most successful librettists and playwrights in Musical Theatre. Any published guide or website dealing with the history of American Theatre will provide you with an overview of his achievements and will almost certainly highlight his collaboration with the composer Jerome Kern in the transformative *Show Boat* (1928) and his later international success in tandem with Richard Rodgers. However, even though it is important for students to know about these works and why they are significant, it is even more vital that they appreciate the quality of the **words** Oscar wrote and why an understanding of them or the words of any other Musical is the **first stage** in working towards any performance and certainly comes **before** singing and dancing.

Task 6

Think about this – in 1964 Richard Rodgers wrote:

> In many ways a song writing partnership is like a marriage. Apart from just liking each other, a lyricist and a composer should be able to spend long periods of time together – around the clock if need be – without getting on each other's nerves. Their goals, outlooks and basic philosophies should be similar.
>
> GUERNSEY, ed. 1964

Take a look at the **words** of any favourite song from a Rodgers and Hammerstein Musical: *Oklahoma!*, *South Pacific* or *The Sound of Music*, perhaps.

Teacher's notes

No, don't introduce the tune yet or sit at the keyboard! Encourage your students to think about every word of the song and identify key words and topics.

You will find that Hammerstein often writes about nature, love and music itself. How are these ideas conveyed? Get your students to speak the words thoughtfully and slowly: emphasizing those words that seem important. For example, how might they speak the line 'Oh, what a beautiful morning! Oh, what a beautiful day!' Experiment with speaking these words truthfully and yet in various ways.

Task 7

Take your students back to Lesson Three, where we mentioned Rodgers and Hammerstein, and introduce the question of which comes first, words or music. Rodgers says:

> 'As a partner he was completely dependable; about 70% of the time I wrote the music only after Oscar handed me the lyric.'

How would you and your students wish to work?

Now ask your students to search for examples in songs by Rodgers and Hammerstein which illustrate the following comment from Richard Rodgers when speaking about Oscar Hammerstein:

'He knew full well that man is not all good and that nature is not all good; yet it was his sincere belief that someone had to keep reminding people of the vast amount of good things in the world.'

GUERNSEY, ed. 1964

Topics for class discussion, student journal entries or essay assignments

1   The 'Broadway' Jewish tradition eventually culminated in a Musical which specifically celebrated that tradition and culture. What Musical was that?

2   Investigate the careers of Rudolph Friml and Sigmund Romberg. Where did they come from and which Musicals made them famous?

3   In which Musicals are the lives of African-Americans portrayed with sympathy and accuracy?

SAMPLE TEST QUESTIONS (MULTIPLE CHOICE):

1   The first slaves from Africa arrived in America in: a) 1920 b) 1619 c)1850 d) 1956.

2   Slaves often worked the fields growing: a) Barley b) Hops for beer c) Cotton d) Coconuts.

3   Jewish tradesmen and musicians came to America in large numbers because of: a) Violence and prejudice towards Jews in their own countries b) Better opportunities in the theatres c) Their attraction to black music d) Their attraction to the film industry.

4   African slaves created songs which borrowed from hymns that postulated the idea of: a) Domination by black races b) Revolution c) The Promised Land d) The Blues.

5   Oscar Hammerstein II often wrote lyrics that celebrated: a) Peace b) The sights and sounds of Nature c) Travellers d) Colonialism.

6   In addition to Richard Rodgers, Hammerstein collaborated with: a) Leonard Bernstein b) Andrew Lloyd Webber c) Jerome Kern d) Lorenz Hart.

7   By the late nineteenth century the number of theatres/opera houses in America was in the region of: a) 500 b) 1000 c) 20,000 d) 5000.

8   Theatres in nineteenth-century Britain and Europe frequently had their own resident: a) Writer b) Builder c) Composer d) Publisher.

9   By the 1940s, the acknowledged capital of the Musical Theatre world was: a) Paris b) Vienna c) London d) New York.

10 In a work of Musical Theatre, the storyline and emotional journey of the characters is conveyed through: a) Choreography b) The integration of acting, singing and dancing c) Speech d) The spectacle of the show.

Reflection: Lesson Six

The title of this lesson was inspired by the memorable choral work by Michael Tippett: *A Child of Our Time*. Written partly as a result of the dreadful events of 'Kristallnacht' in Nazi Germany just before the Second World War, this chilling masterpiece juxtaposes Tippett's own poetic libretto with Spirituals drawn from black culture. It highlights the plight of all those who are compelled to leave their own country by violent forces over which they have no control. Sadly, its theme is as relevant today as when it was first written.

As you consider the issues you have been teaching in this lesson, you may well realize that you have encountered students who trace their families back to Jewish, Irish or African roots or to the victims of colonialism or race-hatred in many parts of the world. The cultural heritage which such people have brought to their new home countries has enriched the development of Musical Theatre in remarkable ways. Students are probably aware of Holocaust history because there have been many films, books and plays that reveal this terrible truth, but they may not be aware of the much earlier antagonism towards Jewish people in Europe, or the facts of black history, or even the reasons why six million Irish people emigrated to the USA in the early years of the twentieth century.

Such gaps in knowledge can make an explanation of the facts we have explored in this lesson difficult. What level of knowledge of these issues did you encounter?

You may wish to ponder as to how the Musicals you have identified as created against a background of dispossession or emigration reflect the traditions from which the writers came. Think of the words of some key Musicals in this genre and contemplate their deeper meaning. Interestingly, Tippett originally hoped that one of the two great poets – T. S. Eliot or W. H. Auden – would write the libretto for *A Child of Our Time* but, after considering his outline for the work, Eliot advised Tippett to write the words himself because he felt that a poet would not be able to create a text that would serve the music in this dramatic but purely sung piece. How does this experience of Tippett's accord with your exploration of the music and lyrics in a Musical?

This is the second lesson in which you will have asked your students to engage with history. How did your work with the previous lesson impact on this lesson? Did you find the students' attitudes more receptive and did they see the relevance of what you were inviting them to investigate? Are there now traditions such as 'Bollywood' which might bring further diversity and creativity to the stage or film Musical?

This lesson will have provided you with an opportunity to encourage students to talk about their own traditions. We vividly remember a student who introduced the class to her tradition in which mothers invariably taught their daughters to cook fajitas. We made a mini Musical from this!

Lesson Seven

'The Biz' – Theatre Examines Itself

Lesson themes

- The world of 'Showbusiness' seems endlessly fascinating: why is this?
- Musical Theatre is often considered the essence of Showbiz
- The Theatre often explores itself in shows. There are many examples and they tell us a great deal about the development of the Theatre and this art form.

Teaching objectives

- To motivate students to participate in activities
- To explore the way in which Theatre examines itself
- To consider examples of shows that reflect aspects of Showbusiness
- To introduce the concept of analysis.

Key facts, teacher notes and in-class activities for students

Stage one: Introducing the topic

Teacher's notes

Students invariably benefit from a 'straight into the work' approach, so we begin with:

Task 1

Sing along to 'There's no Business like Showbusiness', an Irving Berlin song written for the 1946 Musical *Annie Get Your Gun* and sung in the stage show by the members of 'Buffalo Bill's Wild West Show'. It makes an ideal, energetic warm-up for the class: at first hummed and then with the words added.

You might want to let the class hear Ethel Merman's memorable version from the 1954 movie and then sing/dance along.

Teacher's notes

For many students this song epitomises the world of 'Showbusiness' in general and that of Musical Theatre in particular. **Why is this world so endlessly fascinating?**

Task 2

Annie Get Your Gun is only one of many Musicals that explore the nature of Showbiz from the inside. Ask your students to bring/listen to/watch recordings of **or** show clips of: *Show Boat, Kiss Me Kate, A Chorus Line, Cabaret, Sweet Charity, Funny Girl,* or *The Phantom Of The Opera*. Who wrote them and choreographed them, and when?

Stage two: Analysis

At this stage we need to look in more detail at the examples we have given, so here are the key facts about the Musicals cited, which are often referred to as 'back-stage Musicals':

Key facts

- *Show Boat*: book and lyrics by Oscar Hammerstein II, music by Jerome Kern. Based on the novel *Show Boat* by Edner Ferber. First performed New York, 1927

- *Annie Get Your Gun*: book by Dorothy and Herbert Fields, music and lyrics by Irving Berlin. Based on the fictional life of Annie Oakley, the star of 'Buffalo Bill's Wild West Show'. First performed New York, 1946

- *Kiss Me Kate*: book by Sam and Bella Spewack, music and lyrics by Cole Porter. Based on an imaginary performance of a musical version of Shakespeare's *The Taming Of The Shrew*. First performed New York, 1948

- *Funny Girl*: Film Musical with book by Isobel Lennart, lyrics by Bob Merrill, music by Jule Styne. Based on the life of the Broadway performer Fanny Brice. First performed New York, 1964

- *Cabaret*: book by Joe Masteroff, lyrics by Fred Ebb, music by John Kander. Based on John Van Druten's play *I Am A Camera* (1951), which was an adaptation of Christopher Isherwood's novel *Goodbye To Berlin* (1939). First performed New York, 1966

- *Sweet Charity*: book by Neil Simon, lyrics by Dorothy Fields, music by Cy Coleman. Based on the screenplay for the Italian film *Nights Of Cabiria*. First performed New York, 1966

- *A Chorus Line*: book by James Kirkwood and Nicholas Dante, lyrics by Edward Kleban, music by Marvin Hamlisch. Based on the lives of a group of working dancer/performers. First performed New York, 1975

- *The Phantom Of The Opera*: book by Andrew Lloyd Webber and Richard Stilgoe, lyrics by Charles Hart, music by Andrew Lloyd Webber. Based on *Le Fantome de L'Opéra* by Gaston Leroux. First performed London, 1986.

All these Musicals explore, in some ways, aspects of life in the Theatre/ Showbusiness, and many of them have been made into films.

Teacher's notes

If you ever needed evidence of the predominance of Broadway as the home of much Musical Theatre, this list will provide it. You will also notice that we have not given details of the choreographers, even though the dance element was a vital ingredient for all these productions. This is because choreography can change markedly in style and content between productions; but you should notice where the choreography was a distinctive aspect of a production. Bob Fosse's remarkable choreography for *Sweet Charity* is a particularly strong example.

Task 3

Ask your students to focus on one or two Musicals and discover:

a) **What is the cultural context of the work?** Where and when is the action set? Be as specific as possible. For example, for *Cabaret*, an answer might be: 'Set in a night club in 1930s Berlin, when there was a very liberal attitude to sexuality and gender, which was soon to be swept away by the Nazis.'

Teacher's notes

This is what drama scholars might call 'identifying the world of the play' and, of course, in the case of these Musicals there are at least **two** worlds: the 'real' world of politics, events and social conditions and the sometimes 'artificial' world of the Theatre. It is in the interface of these two worlds that much of the interest in these shows lies. Your students may well have followed a TV series in which the intense atmosphere of a Performing Arts school is the setting and enjoyed the 'dramas' that accompany that situation. It is important to appreciate that the Theatre and its accompanying organization provides a somewhat inward-looking world from which some people never escape: at the same time, the Theatre has a responsibility to provide a thoughtful picture of the 'real' world in which the majority of the population have to live and work. Understanding the predicaments of characters in the real world is the next task in this study.

b) **Who are the protagonists?** This term originally came from the Greek Theatre and implied the 'first actor': however, it now it simply means any major character. Make a list of who they are. How old are they? What is their relationship to other characters? What are their circumstances and occupation, what is their role/skill in the world of Theatre? It would be possible to argue that in *A Chorus Line* the entire cast is the protagonist. What is the result of this concept?

Teacher's notes

Dramatic interest is considerably increased when there is tension or symmetry between on and off-stage relationships. This is particularly true of Musicals like *Kiss Me Kate*, in which lovers/partners from 'real life' play the same roles on stage. For many students this may bring up issues of working on stage with those who they like or dislike in real life. This presents you with an opportunity to reinforce professional practice in which personal feelings of affection, rivalry or jealousy have **absolutely no place** in the work of the Theatre. It is healthy and practical to recognize such feelings as rejection, anxiety, excitement or frustrated ambition as they are portrayed in Musicals about the Theatre and to acknowledge that they may form part of your students' work. Indeed, the study of these Musicals may well provide the ideal opportunity for an open and honest discussion of these issues.

Task 4

Divide the class into groups of five or six and then 'hot seat' each member of each group in turn. Every student should take on the role of one of the protagonists they have identified and take turns at being in the centre of the circle, answering questions on their imaginary life. Encourage discussion where a question cannot be answered. This activity should enable you to lead naturally into the Task 5.

Task 5

Ask your students to answer the following questions:

a) **What are the protagonists' predicaments?** Drama is created when the protagonists find themselves in challenging situations. Understanding these situations enables performers to create believable roles and bring a sense of truth to their work. It is essential to identify the various tensions, challenges and pressures that the characters are experiencing in their on- and off-stage lives.

b) **What are the protagonists' goals and drives?** What do they want to achieve? What is stopping them? What are their ambitions? What is the difference between their on-stage performance and their off-stage behaviour?

c) **What picture of life in the Theatre emerges from this show?** How does this compare with your own experience as a way of life? How does contemporary life and Theatre compare with that shown in any one of these Musicals?

d) **What other Musicals, movies or plays can you find which investigate life in the Theatre?** Our list is by no means exhaustive and this is a rich and fascinating area of research. You might begin with David Mamet's short play *A Life In The Theatre* or the movie *Fame*.

Stage three: Practical exploration

Task 6

Now ask your students to find a song from one of the Musicals in our list which seems to encapsulate the central feelings/dilemmas of one of the main protagonists at a key moment in the drama. Ask them to prepare the song for performance, or work in pairs in which one student helps the other to prepare. Remind students of the principles that were established in Lesson Two and extended into Lesson Three. Remind them, too, of the necessity of knowing the writer/composer of the song and the precise context of its origin. Share the results in a non-judgemental and relaxed atmosphere and, in discussion, compare the feelings and experience of the students with those of the characters they are portraying in their acting through song.

Task 7

Group improv: create an imaginary audition/try out scene which explores the inner life of the anxious and hopeful actor/dancer/singer. What song might they select to show themselves at their best? How would they use accompaniment? What are the emotions involved in this entire process? As a teacher you will need to spread yourself among the groups. Notice where a group's attention might be flagging or if some group members are too dominant in discussion. Be ready to supply or find a source of technical help with sound/keyboard etc.

Teacher's notes

Show and share the improv. The cast must agree what line the various 'panel' members will take. 'Audience' questions from the rest of the group: only 'OK' questions allowed: find something positive to say or ask.

Stage four: Going deeper

Another 'back-stage' Musical which rewards close attention is *42nd Street*. The show has a particularly fascinating stage history and genesis and rewards research. The internet will supply copious information about the location of the action and its context, together with details of the plot.

Here, however, are the **key facts**:

- *42nd Street*: book by Michael Stewart and Mark Bramble, lyrics by Al Dublin and Johnny Mercer, music by Harry Warren. Based on the novel *42nd Street* (1932) by Bradford Ropes and the Hollywood film version of the same name (1933)
- The show also has aspects of 'jukebox Musical' because, in addition to songs from the 1933 film *42nd Street*, it includes songs that Dubin and Warren wrote for many other films during the same period.

Now we revisit some of our earlier tasks.

Task 7

a) What is the cultural context of the work?
This leads us to many other questions: for example, what is the significance of the title? 42nd Street is a street in New York that intersects with Broadway in Times Square. It is situated in the heart of theatre-land and had a reputation for being part of the 'red light' district. As Harwood (1984) so vividly put it, the area has usually:

a floating population of pimps and whores, winos and junkies, unkempt policemen, street vendors and street musicians, eccentrics and derelicts,

as well as conventional people going about their conventional business
and sightseers going about theirs.

255

Indeed, the show itself describes this environment in one of its early songs:

> Where the underworld can meet the elite
> Naughty, gawdy, bawdy, sporty, Forty-second Street.

Teacher's notes

It may seem remarkable that so much information can emerge from simply examining
the significance of a title, but this is the essence of what we are suggesting. Far too
many students simply take a song from a show or ask to perform a dance number
from it without any real understanding of what the work is about.

Further questions on cultural context

Where, precisely, is the action taking place?

The action takes place in a theatre which is preparing to present a show
called *Pretty Lady*, so, like *Kiss Me Kate*, we are in the world of performance.
The auditions for parts in the show are nearly completed. We soon discover
that much of the effect of the intended performance is based on tap dancing
and the extensive use of a glamorous chorus of girls.

Perhaps, more significantly: **when** is the action taking place? The answer
is 1933: at the height of the Great Depression in the USA. This terrible
period in world history began in 1929 with a huge economic downturn in
the US, which spread to the rest of the Western world. It is well worth our
spending some time researching the effect of these events on people's
attitudes and behaviour in order to bring some authenticity and truth to the
exploration of *42nd Street*. The key issue is what mounting a show like
Pretty Lady was attempting to achieve: escapism, comfort for the 'tired
businessman' (as *The Follies* had been) or sheer defiance? All the protagonists
in the work are affected by these issues; so we consider them now:

b) Who are the protagonists?

We can begin by looking at the cast list provided by the agents for the show
and in the libretto:

- **Peggy Sawyer (Lead)** – Nervous but enthusiastic new chorus girl
  from Allentown Pennsylvania
- **Billy Lawlor (Lead)** – Leading tenor in *Pretty Lady*
- **Dorothy Brock (Lead)** – Past her prime Prima Donna, renowned for
  inability to dance
- **Julian Marsh (Lead)** – Famous, but notorious, director
- **Maggie Jones (Support)** – Co-writer and producer of *Pretty Lady*

- **Bert Barry (Support)** – Co-writer and producer of *Pretty Lady*
- **Andy Lee (Support)** – Choreographer/Dance Director
- **Pat Denning (Support)** – Dorothy's former vaudeville partner and romantic interest
- **Abner Dillon (Support)** – Producer of *Pretty Lady*; Dorothy's 'Sugar Daddy' and Texan admirer
- **Mac (Support)** – Stage Manager
- **Ann 'Anytime Annie' Reilly, Lorraine Flemming, Phyllis Dale, and Gladys (Support)** – Experienced chorus girls who help Peggy
- **Oscar** – On-stage rehearsal pianist for the show *Pretty Lady*
- **Doctor**
- **Other small speaking roles** (Thugs, waiter, etc.)
- **Large Tap/Chorus Ensemble**

We can note that there are four characters listed as 'leads', and these certainly are the main protagonists, but, as we pointed out in Lesson Five, the chorus may itself be a protagonist and it is important to keep its central role in this Musical in mind.

Task 8

Ask your students to study this list carefully until they have grasped the situations, relationships, roles and responsibilities. How do the lives of these people in the Theatre relate to their lives **outside** the Theatre? Notice, for instance, that Peggy already has a 'back story' because she has newly arrived but some of the other characters seem only to exist in the 'world of the Theatre'.

Task 9

Having identified the main protagonists, now ask your students to identify their **stories**. Theatre only works well if it tells a story or stories and so it is vital to grasp the **plot** of the show. As students do this, revert to the earlier questions:

c) What are the protagonists' predicaments?
We take Peggy as an example.

Peggy is newly arrived and unsure of herself. When she encounters Billy, who has already been cast in the show, she learns that she is too late for the audition but that he, in an attempt to charm her, might be able to get her a part.

She is immediately in a dilemma: can she trust Billy? Can she resist his advances?

When she meets the choreographer, Andy, her worst fears are realized: Billy's offer is worthless and she is humiliated by Andy's reprimand. Her predicament becomes intense when, already demoralized and embarrassed, she encounters the director, Julian.

Peggy is befriended by some other chorus girls and shows them a dance routine that is also seen by the director: even though she is now offered a part in the show she, inevitably, feels uncertain of herself and wishes that she had obtained the part by a more conventional route.

All this is set against the normal tensions caused by the approach of an 'opening' but made far worse by the non-arrival of the scenery and costumes, the complex personal relationships and mis-casting among the performers and the shifting attitudes towards her by various members of the cast and production team.

Teacher's notes

These notes are merely an example of the preparatory work that is needed before any attempt at performance of an extract, song or scene from the show.

d) What are the protagonists' goals and drives?

If we again focus on Peggy we might suggest that, in the light of what we have noted above, her main goal is 'survival'! We can see that she has a burning ambition to perform but, as the plot unfolds, she has to modify her behaviour to cope with the advances of both Billy and Julian. She must avoid alienating other members of the chorus by allowing Julian's admiration to make them jealous and eventually has to endure the shock of both being fired from the production and being enticed to return. Her goals constantly shift but she never loses the drive to perform. She has to square this with her feeling of disillusionment that drives her to tell Julian she has had enough of Showbusiness!

Stage five: Into performance

Task 10

With your particular group of students in mind, select one or two of the following songs from *42nd Street* and help them to learn it: 'Young and Healthy','Go into your Dance', 'Lullaby of Broadway', 'Getting Out of Town'.

Begin your preparation with the questions: 'Who are you? Where are you? What is happening to you?' Then work on the singing/performance.

Task 12

Hot-seat members of your groups, asking them to prepare one of the following roles, in the character of which they must respond to questions: Dorothy, Julian, Peggy, Pat, Abner, Andy.

Topics for class discussion, student journal entries and essay assignments

1   Think back to lesson one: what understanding now informs and supports your performance?

2   Find a song which seems to capture some of the essential dilemmas and challenges of a performer. Perhaps compare this with David Mamet's play *A Life In The Theatre* or one of Chekhov's short plays about being an actor.

3   What picture of life in the Theatre emerges from the shows introduced during the teaching session? What is the essence of being a performer and how do these Musicals work as biographies/ autobiographies?

4   Which of these 'back-stage' Musicals come nearest to your own experience of the Theatre?

5   What particular feature of *42nd Street* caused audiences to applaud when the initial curtain went up? Why do you think the audience responded in this way?

6   Why does the Theatre seem to constantly examine itself in public?

SAMPLE TEST QUESTIONS (MULTIPLE CHOICE)

1   The major protagonists in a Musical are sometimes called:
a) Principals b) Leads c) Starters d) Stars.

2   The cultural context of *Cabaret*: a) The Great Depression
b) Broadway c) 1930s Berlin d) Dublin.

3   One of the major problems for the cast of *42nd Street* is: a) Poor lighting b) Injury to a performer c) The dressing rooms d) Negative critical response.

4   *A Chorus Line* is highly successful in portraying: a) Production problems b) The difficulties of working with an accompanist c) The behaviour of directors d) The professional and personal lives of performers.

5   'Back-stage' Musicals show: a) Life in the live theatre b) The private lives of directors c) Staging conditions in old theatres d) Stage machinery.

6 The characters in *Kiss Me Kate* are preparing a musical version of a play by: a) Harold Pinter b) Rodgers and Hammerstein c) William Shakespeare d) Hal Prince.

7 The characters in *42nd Street* are preparing a show called: a) Pretty Boy b) Pretty Woman c) The Boyfriend d) Pretty Lady.

8 *Show Boat* was a collaboration between the librettist Oscar Hammerstein II and: a) Richard Rodgers b) Leonard Bernstein c) Jerome Kern d) Andrew Lloyd Webber.

9 *The Phantom Of The Opera* was first produced in: a) New York b) Berlin c) Paris d) London.

10 The main protagonist in *Sweet Charity* is: a) An actor b) A choreographer c) A dancer d) A charity worker.

Reflection: Lesson Seven

What did you discover about the expectations and experience of your students from this lesson? Had any of them been seduced by TV shows that dramatized or glorified the life of the Theatre or did they identify with characters in one of the shows you mentioned?

Students rarely opt to study Musical Theatre unless they have acquired an early passion for performance. This lesson will have provided an opportunity for you to discover how they relate imaginatively to the characters and situations in the Musicals which form the content of the lesson. How did they draw upon their previous experience in order to bring truthfulness to their approach to the various works you explored?

Following this lesson, it would benefit your approach to the remaining lessons if you were to reflect on why **you** think that Showbusiness finds it necessary to examine itself so frequently and publicly. Is it a sense of constant insecurity or emotional craving? Is it because life in the Theatre is so stressful or so precarious? Is it because it is so rewarding and creative that it 'feeds the soul' as Dr Faustus said in Marlowe's play?

Make a careful mental note of all that you observed in this lesson: especially recall the students' approach to understanding the predicaments of the characters. If you think back to the lesson in which you were demanding that students **speak** the words of the text of songs in order to appreciate the subtext, you will see how exercises in which they think about the inner lives of the characters will add to the quality of their performances.

This lesson may have been a reminder to you of what students have committed to do. Their contemporaries who have elected to study more passive or private subjects may have very different challenges or opportunities. Visual arts students hang their pictures on the wall, creative writing students print their creative writing in a book; history students create essays or mount presentations; Theatre students hang themselves on the wall and **are** the book from which the observer reads!

In a University in the USA a student was overheard announcing at the point at which a choice of 'major' subjects had to be made: 'It's official, I'm a freak, I'm a theatre major!' How would you account for such a statement in the light of your experience?

An awareness of the unique demands of our discipline may well mean that we come to know students far better than other teachers do, and this lesson enables you to reflect on the artistic and personal support we give to students. It also reminds us of the professional boundaries we must observe to ensure that our attention is equally spread.

We would recommend that, as a complementary activity, you read the autobiographies of some leading performers or other Theatre practitioners. Consider how meetings and interactions affected their careers. All too often these are stories of people who are the centre of their own universe but, equally, they are stories of how a single word transformed a life.

Lesson Eight

Chorus Time – 'Do You Hear the People Sing?'

Lesson themes

This lesson concentrates on the idea of a chorus in Musical Theatre and all that the name implies. Students tend to feel disappointed if they are cast as members of a chorus and will even suggest that they have been given an 'insignificant opportunity' because they are '**only** in the chorus'. Always be quick to remind your students that: 'There is no such thing as an "insignificant" role, only "insignificant actors"'! That word 'only' is totally inappropriate in this context, but students need to be made aware of the vital contribution that a chorus makes to a production.

Teaching objectives

- To enable students to appreciate the value of the chorus in Musical Theatre
- To establish some of the vital history and ideas of development of the chorus
- To explore examples of imaginative use of the chorus
- Explore the genre and different styles involved in Musical Theatre.

Key facts, teacher's notes and in-class activities for Students

Stage one: The concept

Key facts

Before beginning any work on the chorus itself, it is a good idea to consider the differing qualities that the chorus might bring to a Musical in order to establish the community in which the action takes place. Examples will range from hoofers (*A Chorus Line*) to Russian peasants (*Fiddler On The Roof*) to a ragged company of players (*Pippin*), plus many other Musicals that consider specific groups of people, such as: visitors (*Grand Hotel*); film personalities and crew (*Sunset Boulevard*), a stage company (*Curtains*), travellers across oceans (*Anything Goes*), a collection of feline characters (*Cats*), a pride of lions (*The Lion King*), a set of gang members (*West Side Story*), citizens in a community (*Urine Town*), prisoners and murderers (*Chicago*) or a set of night club workers (*Le Cage Aux Folles* or *Taboo*). The list is almost endless. The narratives they tell are varied yet the atmospheres they create are essential to the overall impact of the Musicals themselves! Without the chorus the narrative becomes stark and bare and although in some Musicals the absence of a chorus is a key feature, in most situations the chorus brings vibrancy and colour to the genre.

Task 1

A good task to start:

   Identify a Musical or a 'revue' which has significant chorus roles from each decade of the twentieth century. Name them and suggest what contribution the chorus makes to the overall narrative of the Musical.

Key facts

Like so many words in Theatre, the term 'chorus' has its origins in Ancient Greece and, of course, it also includes the origin of the term 'choreography': the movement of that chorus. The term invariably implies doing something together, but it also suggests 'storytellers' and it has been known for a single chorus figure to fulfil that purpose.

   In Musical Theatre the role of the chorus has become central to the popularity and success of the genre. We now expect the chorus to be highly disciplined and skilled: frequently able to sing, dance and act – 'triple threat', with the same level of expertise. You might think that talent is enough but in the days of the *Ziegfeld Follies* your height, as in ballet, was a significant factor in your employment.

The girls were identified by their height as follows:

5'7"	Tall girls – Showgirls (front line)
5'5"–5'7"	Peaches – speciality dancers with tricks and gimmicks to perform
5'2"–5'6"	Chickens
5'–5'5"	Ponies
5'–5'3"	Pacers

In some historic forms of Musical Theatre, like 'revue', the chorus was little more than an excuse for glamour, and, to some extent, this remains true of certain shows. From the middle of the last century onwards there has been a far greater focus on 'ensemble' playing in the Theatre; the famous Berliner Ensemble of Bertolt Brecht, for example, established a system totally devoid of 'stars' and was devoted to collaboration and equality amongst the cast. Musicals dating from the period of Brecht's influence, especially those of Andrew Lloyd Webber and Tim Rice, place a strong emphasis on using the chorus for multiple roles. For instance, the entire male and female cast of Cole and Pickering's Rock Musical *Ulysses* (a dramatic retelling of Homer's *Odyssey*) begin by re-enacting the siege of Troy in song and dance. The men then become the crew of a ship whilst the women become, in sequence: sirens, lotus eaters, Circe's helpers, sheep, the helpers of the Cyclops and witnesses at the final archery contest to win Penelope's hand. The men, having endured a succession of trials and temptations, become the competitors in the archery contest, whilst every now and again one of the 'chorus' emerges to play a lead role for a scene and then returns to the relative anonymity of the chorus. In shows like this, 'chorus' members are given solo singing moments and yet are also required to master every singing, acting and dancing demand of the ensemble. As we shall see in a later lesson, the role of the chorus as a major character in itself reached its peak in Hamlisch and Kleban's *A Chorus Line* (1975)

However, the level of involvement, commitment and focus that we now expect from a chorus was not always the case; for example, in the nineteenth century the great composer Hector Berlioz complained in his 'memoirs' that the choruses in Opera Houses spent their time gossiping, flirting and paying little attention during rehearsals! We owe a great deal to the nineteenth-century playwright and director W. S. Gilbert for bringing a new sense of discipline and purpose to the Musical Theatre, and he left very precise instructions for the movements, reactions and behaviour of the chorus in the operettas he wrote with the composer Arthur Sullivan. We shall encounter the work of Gilbert and Sullivan in a subsequent lesson.

Teacher's notes

Even though you have used and applied the ideas contained in Lesson Four, it is quite possible that you might find the prospect of teaching this lesson somewhat intimidating, especially if you have little dance experience or choreographic knowledge: do not be discouraged! You may well find that you have a student with substantial dance experience who would be happy to devise some simple choreography, or there are many simple exercises that can build upon the basic idea of 'choreography' as 'movement of the chorus'. Indeed, some of the most successful Musicals currently playing on Broadway or in other major city venues contain choreography that was originally devised through improvisation. Go back to Lesson Four to boost your confidence.

Stage two: Recognizing the styles

Teacher's notes

It is important, however, for students to gain an insight into the role and development of the chorus in Musical Theatre, because this is an integral part of their understanding. Shows with a huge variety of choreographic styles remain popular. It would be useful for your students to research and find out a little about significant choreographers of the Musical, including Julian Mitchell, Busby Berkeley, Bobby Alton and Sammy Lee, before investigating the influence of Agnes de Mille, with her ground-breaking choreography of *Oklahoma!*. She was known for her unique achievements within the musical genre by integrating dance with the acting and singing. Subsequently, the nature of the dance has increasingly established the style and atmosphere of shows. So, whether it is by watching movie versions, live streaming or actual productions of works or experimenting with the choreographic potential of a particular song, it is important to expose students to the range of chorus work now available. Other choreographers to investigate following on from the work of Agnes de Mille would be George Balanchine, John Tiller and the Tiller Girls, Jerome Robbins, Bob Fosse, Michael Bennett and Susan Stroman to name but a few.

Task 3

Compare the chorus of *Ziegfeld Follies*; *42nd Street* and *A Chorus Line*.

1 What are the qualities of movement in the opening numbers?
2 What is the role of each member of the chorus?
3 How do these three shows demonstrate a line of development in thinking about the chorus?
4 If you have the skill/time try out a section of these numbers. What did the students learn from the experience?
5 How are the stories told through the chorus?
6 How did events such as the 'crash' of 1929, the Prohibition and Depression impact upon the form and structure of Musical Theatre in America?

7 When do members of the chorus begin to have names and identities? How important is this to the development of Musical Theatre and the role of the chorus?

8 What was the impact of the Mega-Musical of the 1980s on the chorus identity?

9 Identify three choreographers and what each of them contributed to the genre of Musical Theatre.

10 Can you identify the types of girl dancers and see how and where they fit into the routines?

Task 4

If your own or the class experience is not appropriate to attempting to perform an extract from these shows, rely on watching movie/recorded versions of them and discuss the issues raised and/or try the following exercise:

1 Find a simple recording of music with a clear, slow 1, 2, 3 rhythm.

2 Divide the class into groups of 4.

3 One member of the group must devise and teach a sequence of three simple movements to the rest of the group: one of the movements must involve progress by a step across the floor.

4 The whole group then learns the sequence and rehearses so that they move in 'sync' with each other. Repeat until the sequence becomes almost second nature.

Task 5

Look into dances on video or tabulated descriptions of the 'Turkey Trot' or the 'Black Bottom' and learn them as a routine. Then invent a scene where you could incorporate one of these routines into the storyline. Let your students realize that the social dances of the day are an important aspect of training for Musical Theatre, and so long as they are willing to learn the steps, there are opportunities in Musical Theatre for non-dancers! The original male chorus members in early Musicals were not dancers; they were just very aware of the social dance of the day and had a good time at the various night clubs in town.

Task 6

Create a current dance routine by inventing a scene and performing your own contemporary Musical Theatre video using 'moves' of today. Think of Madonna or Michael Jackson.

Stage three: Singing

Key facts

If we return once more to the Greeks we might consider a play such as *Oedipus Rex*. Identify the role of the chorus: where they are on stage and what they represent. Often, they are seated or positioned in a semi-circle and facing the auditorium. They might represent the various aspects of city life – if there are two factions then the chorus would be split and be identified as having contrasting qualities. These might include roles as citizens, the audience, the scene setters (as in the Theatre of Brecht) and most importantly, the tellers of the story being enacted by the main protagonists. The Greek chorus had significant responsibility in terms of the overall structure and form of the play in much the same way as the chorus has in Musical Theatre. In Greek drama the chorus had the 'responsibility' for (i) 'taking sides and sharing their intentions with the audience, (ii) analysing the situation and explaining it to their audience, (iii) anticipating the action in terms of warning of an event, (iv) telling the audience what is happening as the storyteller and (v) adding 'colour' and atmosphere to the event like, for example, describing the thunder and lightning relating to the anger of the Gods!

Task 7

Choose a simple folk song with a strong narrative. For example: 'Little Sir William'. Work in groups to present the story as a piece of Greek drama using the skills of the 'chorus' to communicate the narrative. Make it as dramatic and exciting as you can!

Little Sir William

Easter day was a holiday
Of all days of the year
And all the little schoolfellows went out to play
But Sir William was not there

Mamma went to the School wife house
And knocked at the ring
Saying, 'Little Sir William, if you are there
Pray let your mother in.'

The School wife opened the door and said:
'He is not here today
He is with the little schoolfellows out on the green
Playing some pretty play.'

Mamma went to the Boyne water
That is so wide and deep

Saying, 'Little Sir William, if you are there
Oh pity your mother's weep.'

'How can I pity your weep, mother
And I so long in pain?
For the little pen knife sticks close to my heart
And the School wife hath me slain

'Go home, go home, my mother dear
And prepare my winding sheet
For tomorrow morning before eight o'clock
You with my body shall meet.'

LITTLE SIR WILLIAM

Somerset Folk Song

Bright ♩ = 100   rall.

a tempo
CHORUS

East - er day was a hol - i - day of all days of the year.   And all the

2

lit - tle school fel-lows went out to play, but Sir Will - iam was not there.

Mam - ma went to the School wife's house and knocked at the ring. Say-ing

3

4

with the lit-tle school fel-lows out   on the green,__ play-ing some pret - ty   play.

Flt   rall.

Meno mosso ♩ = 85
CHORUS

Mam - ma   went   to the Boy — ne wat-er that is   so   wide   and   deep,   say-ing,

p

MAMMA

"Lit-tle Sir   Will - 'am,   if   you are there,   oh   pit - y   your moth - er's   weep."

5

Much slower ♩ = 75
LITTLE SIR WILLIAM

"How can I pi - ty your weep, moth-er and I so long in pain? For the

CHORUS

lit - tle pen knife sticks close to his heart and the School wife hath he slain.

a tempo

LITTLE SIR WILLIAM

"Go

6

home. go home, my moth - er dear and pre - pare my wind ing

CHORUS

sheet." For to - mor-ow morn-ing be - fore eight o' clock she

rall.

will his bo - dy shall meet.

Task 8

1 Learn the simple melody and then in groups, identify a way of
   performing the story with actions and commentary in much the
   same way as a Greek chorus.

2 Identify the main protagonists in the narrative and find moments
   when they can enter and leave the performance space with the
   chorus commenting upon the action.

3 Try to find ways in which the performance ensemble incorporates all
   five points of 'responsibility' as mentioned above.

4   This will require the group to not only sing the chorus or speak it as appropriate but to be able to tell the story, predict the action and, where necessary, change the scene.

Recordings and YouTube performances of folk songs are available if required.

Stage four: Deepening the understanding

Key facts

We move rapidly through the centuries, from the treatment of the simple folk song relating to Greek drama to 1728 and *The Beggar's Opera* by John Gay, which was also connected to 'ballads' and 'popular songs': potentially a 'Jukebox Musical' of the day! This musical ran for a good number of performances in London (146) mainly because the music was known to the audiences and everyone could sing along: much like a sing-along *Mamma Mia* or even *The Rocky Horror Show*. No longer did the chorus have to inform the audience of the narrative, as the audience members were familiar with the plot line and recognized the characters being portrayed as characters in their own society. It was not surprising that when this Musical was revived in 1920 it ran for 1463 performances – a great commercial success. *The Beggar's Opera* remains one of the greatest influences on Musical Theatre today.

Following on from this revival in 1928, two giants of twentieth-century Theatre, Bertolt Brecht and Kurt Weill, collaborated on a Musical entitled *The Threepenny Opera*. The storyline Brecht followed remained similar, but the music was rewritten and composed by Kurt Weill. Unfortunately, the success of the Musical was the cause of one of the greatest 'splits' in collaborative work in the Theatre, as Brecht was furious that the music gained more popularity than the words. He soon stopped working with Weill to go his own way and write his own music when needed!

Task 9

1) To capture this period in the development of Musical Theatre, look at both *The Beggar's Opera* and *The Threepenny Opera*.

2) Find a scene in *The Beggar's Opera* that suits the number of performers you have in a group. Then find the equivalent scene for *The Threepenny Opera*.

3) Playing the same characters in both scenes, rehearse and perform both scenes in a performance style you think is appropriate to the Musical. Remember that the audience would know all the music in *The Beggar's Opera* but would not be familiar with the music of Kurt Weill. How would this impact upon the performance and performers?

4) Having performed the two scenes to each other, discuss what you discovered about the two Musicals in terms of telling the story, use of chorus (if any), treatment of characters, staging and style of performance.

Teacher's notes

Encourage your students to write a short reflective piece about the discoveries made whilst working on these two scenes. **Do not wait until the performance has been completed.**

Stage five: Into performance

Key facts

The establishment of equality between male and female dancers within Musical Theatre was a struggle in the early 1900s. African-American performers experienced similar problems of discrimination. Work on the chorus provides a good opportunity to explore not only gender balance in the chorus work of early Musicals but also the role of famous African-American performers who contributed to Black Musical Theatre.

Bill 'Bojangles' Robinson was one such artist who established himself in a Musical Theatre world that was intolerant of and hostile to such an intrusion. It would be relevant at this point to consider the song about him and create a chorus number.

[Suggested Song: 'Mr Bojangles']

Task 10

Ask your students to:

1   Listen to a few versions of the song. Write reflective notes on the different qualities each singer brings to the song. What do you like or dislike? Why?

2   Now perform the song and identify how, as an individual performer, you would deliver the story to an audience. Speak and sing moments where relevant.

3   Divide the song between two people who have the same story to tell and establish a reason why, through your performance. Create your own scenario.

4   Now, using four singers, establish a small chorus number to tell the story of this famous performer – use spoken and sung techniques to make the work effective.

5   Before continuing, now listen to the 'Cell Block Tango' from *Chicago* and see how the chorus of girls each tell their own story?

6   Now, in a similar style, use the music and the lyrics and create your own Musical Theatre scene using these lyrics to honour this famous performer.

7   Identify your character and your reason to sing about this character: mother, friend, brother, teacher, lover, director etc. Make your work individual but still part of an overall narrative to provide the impact of the chorus.

Task 11

Look with your students at 'Gee Officer Krupke' from *West Side Story* and set them the following challenge:

1   Study the film version of *West Side Story*.

2   Describe the setting in the original production on film.

3   Establish and discuss the 'belief systems' and the social values of both gangs. What is it that binds each gang together?

4   Identify a contemporary setting for your performance work and rehearse the 'Gee Officer Krupke' sequence.

5   Recreate a contemporary movement style for the presentation.

6   Identify an imaginary history for each character played within the scene.

7   What do you think this chorus scene communicates to a contemporary audience in terms of trust, loyalty, social and cultural ideas?

Task 12

Work with the class on performing 'Do you Hear the People Sing' from *Les Misérables*.

1   Gather the entire group together.

2   Discuss the situation of the song and what it means to each individual person on stage.

Ask them to:

1   Discover their inner life and find ways to present this through the chorus action.

2   Understand their place and positioning on stage and why they are there.

3   Know who the other people are. Not colleagues in a rehearsal, but people in Paris who they work and eat with, or even dislike.

4   Establish a situation for all the people near you on stage. Make the
    action happen.

After several rehearsals and constant challenges as to why your students do
what they do and take the actions they do, the song will come to life and
they will at last realize how important the chorus is as individuals and as an
ensemble.

Topics for class discussion, student journal entries or essay assignments

1   Consider the chorus in the Rock Musical *Jesus Christ Superstar*,
    which begins with the words 'What's the buzz, tell me what's
    happening.' A crowd of people, each with differing expectations, is
    awaiting the arrival of Jesus. Characters sing the chorus and various
    individuals have small 'solo' moments, often only one line of sung
    dialogue. How do they perform this? What are their movements as
    they sing the entire chorus? How does this chorus contribute to the
    total drama and action?

2   The 'dancing' in this number may well appear to be very individual
    and could begin with free improvization. How can this build into a
    cohesive performance?

3   Once the class has worked on creating a truthful scene, introduce
    the arrival of Jesus and his disciples: how do these 'characters' relate
    to the chorus members?

4   If students decided to dance in this scene, what style did they use
    and how was this shaped by the music or context of the scene? Only
    when they have completed the experiments should they take some
    time to view a recorded or movie version of the show.

SAMPLE TEST QUESTIONS (MULTIPLE CHOICE)

1   A major early contributor to an understanding of the importance of
    the chorus was: a) Tim Rice b) W. S. Gilbert c) Leonard Bernstein d)
    Hal Prince.

2   The role of the chorus may be: a) to comment on the main action b)
    provide glamour c) to provide a 'crowd' d) all of these.

3 The opening chorus of *42nd Street* is notable for its: a) jazz dance b) dream ballet c) tap dancing d) hip-hop.

4 The chorus in *West Side Story* creates the sense of: a) harmonious community b) rival gangs c) bored teenagers d) peace.

5 Black performers in early Musical Theatre experienced: a) favoured positions b) discrimination c) star billing d) equal rights with other performers.

6 Brecht and Weill found future collaboration difficult after: a) the failure of their *Threepenny Opera* b) disputes over the chorus c) the outstanding success of the music d) critical remarks.

7 The term 'chorus' has its origins in: a) Gilbert and Sullivan b) Ancient Greece c) Brecht's work d) A Musical by Kleban.

8 A crowd of people expecting the arrival of Jesus is part of the musical: a) *Godspell* b) *Hair* c) *Jesus Christ Superstar* d) *A Chorus Line*.

9 In the *Ziegfeld Follies* the dancers were identified by their: a) voices b) characters c) height d) weight.

10 *The Beggar's Opera* was written in the: a) twentieth century b) fifteenth century c) eighteenth century d) seventeenth century.

Reflection: Lesson Eight

Stanislavsky wrote: 'There are no small parts, only small actors.' Reflect on that phrase; investigate and continue to discuss what he might have meant by that statement if applied to the world of Musical Theatre. Often, the chorus members think that no-one is watching them and so they appear to move with no purpose, characters have little depth and no reason for being there and, even more troubling, they actually watch the action as observers rather than being '*in the action*'. There is so much to do! If Stanislavsky should be remembered for one thing it is the fact that he created a company where everyone is equal in telling their part of the story. This must be so in working in the chorus. How successful were you in helping the students to grasp this concept?

Think about the Musicals discovered whilst preparing and teaching this lesson and identify how rich each Musical is in social, cultural, artistic and political ideas and commentaries. How does each chorus member contribute to these issues?

A good future discussion point or a task would be to choose ONE Musical that you know well and see how it might work without a chorus? Try to identify what happens to the overall narrative when the chorus is no longer present to support the action. As we write, there are strict rules on 'social distancing' which make this a realistic possibility!

It is important for students to understand that chorus work is often seen as having a *'small part'* and thus *'not being good enough to take the main role'*. Nothing is further from the truth! It takes a great skill to be effective in the chorus: it is the entire world of the Musical. Each movement and aspect of physicality must be meaningful for the universal mood being reflected by the chorus. In *Hamilton* the choreographer, Andy Blankenbuehler, identifies the importance of every lyric sung by the chorus and creates choreographic moves based on the lyrics. The detail is significant, and the integrity of the chorus is extreme. How successful were you in conveying these ideas in this lesson? How can a choreographer take lyrics and replicate them in physical movement? If we explore the idea of 'stylized' movement does each lyric have movement potential?

Did your students understand the full implication of the chorus? Did they come to realize what fun it is to be in the chorus? If you feel that you achieved neither of these outcomes, we suggest that for a future task you ask them to take a short section of a chorus from any Musical and then:

Select the lyrics and discover a dynamic movement for each word. Rehearse slowly and then let each word follow through with the movement, remembering to use the whole body, not just the hands. Then speed the movements and lyric up to the pace of the chorus. Finally add the accompaniment. Now the students will be starting to experience how Andy Blankenbuehler works in order to create a chorus in action. They can be as inventive as possible with their actions and as literal as they want!

A final future word of advice to your students regarding chorus work should be:

- Never **COUNT** your lines as a sign of how important you are to the production
- Make your lines **COUNT** in terms of expressing the ideas of the production.

Lesson Nine

Patter to Rap

Lesson themes

This lesson introduces students to one of the most remarkable and influential creative duos in the history of Musical Theatre: Gilbert and Sullivan.

The work of the playwright and librettist W. S. Gilbert and the composer Arthur Sullivan was once so popular that almost every community or amateur Theatre company would include one of their 'comic operas' in their repertoire and the productions of Gilbert and Sullivan by the D'Oyly Carte company were almost legendary. The content of Gilbert and Sullivan's works has influenced the development of Musical Theatre ever since and they are still worth performing and exploring.

The 'patter song' so brilliantly exploited by Gilbert and Sullivan now has its successor in rap.

Teaching objectives

- To interest students in the work of Gilbert and Sullivan
- To explore their techniques and achievements
- To show how later generations have benefitted from their innovations and reforms
- To encourage creative approaches to works written in an earlier period of history
- To establish links with contemporary Musicals and techniques.

Key facts, teacher's notes and in-class activities for students

Stage one: Introducing the subject

Key facts

Gilbert and Sullivan were at the height of their popularity in the late Victorian era in London, but their fame spread to the USA and other parts of the English-speaking world. For many years, the productions of Gilbert and Sullivan's works were governed by the precise, copyrighted stage directions devised by Gilbert, who directed all the premieres of the shows he wrote with Sullivan. Gilbert was particularly concerned with the action of the chorus, which he directed with strict discipline and precision. We have already seen how ill-disciplined the chorus could be at that time. However, since the 1970s, when the copyright of the stage directions expired, directors have been free to interpret the text in any way they wish and this has resulted in some varied, imaginative and progressive productions that are well worth exploring. You might, for example, look at Jonathan Miller's remarkable production of *The Mikado*, which reset the action from Japan to a London Hotel in the 1930s!

Gilbert was notable for being so anxious on opening nights that he could not bring himself to watch the performance. This trait, together with his sometimes stormy relationship with Sullivan, is the subject of Mike Leigh's movie *Topsy Turvy*.

Arthur Sullivan was a leading orchestral composer in his own right and many of his pieces (including well-known hymn tunes) have survived. W. S. Gilbert also enjoyed an independent career as a playwright, but it was in co-operation with each other that these creative artists achieved such success. Their 'operettas' or 'comic operas' (as they became known) such as *Iolanthe*, *The Mikado*, *The Pirates Of Penzance* and *The Gondoliers* were rich in glorious tunes, memorable rhythms and witty lyrics.

Stage two: Looking deeper

More key facts

What were their works about?
Almost all of Gilbert and Sullivan's operettas take well-known 'institutions' and make fun of them! These institutions include the police, the law, the armed forces, the church and the arts. Other targets for their wit and satire are popular trends in fashion and other aspects of contemporary behaviour. Gilbert and Sullivan would often take a national event and build a narrative around it: for example, in 1885–7 there was a Japanese exhibition in London that brought details of a completely unknown culture to the attention of the

public. Gilbert and Sullivan responded with *The Mikado*, which is set in Japan. The movements of the chorus, the costume and set designs, were all based on designs seen on Japanese screens and vases and the music used intervals and motifs derived from some of the Japanese music heard at the exhibition.

Task 1

Ask your students to listen to a recording of *The Mikado* and identify a musical number that is clearly based on Japanese music.

Task 2

Challenge the group to identify what is being satirized in any two of the comic operas mentioned in this chapter.

Task 3

Research the fan movements that might be appropriate for the opening chorus of *The Mikado* and then teach them to the entire group.

Task 4

One of Gilbert's favourite techniques was the 'patter song'. This consisted of a rapidly delivered monologue virtually spoken to music. In performance the patter song demands good breath control and perfect articulation. The text was invariably rhymed and humorous and, in the hands of a gifted actor/singer, patter songs form a highlight in a production. Examples to work on include 'I've Got a Little List' from *The Mikado* and 'I Am the Very Model of a Modern Major General' from *The Pirates Of Penzance*. Ask your students to try them!

Stage three: Into the modern world

A modern realization

When the famous Theatre director, Dr Jonathan Miller (d.2019), decided to work on *The Mikado* in 1986, he changed the setting entirely so that the action, originally set in Japan, was located in a seaside hotel in the 1930s which was visited by a Japanese delegation. The choreography was entrusted to a chorus of waiters and waitresses and included a whole range of jazz and modern dance techniques. There was no obvious attempt to reproduce the now dated attitudes towards another culture, but every opportunity was taken to make modern, even contemporary references (including, in a very recent version, to President Trump). The 'little list' patter song was re-written to include many individuals from modern life who 'would not be missed'!

Fortunately, Miller's remarkable production has been preserved on film and serves as a good example of what he meant when he referred to giving Theatre works 'an afterlife'.

Task 5

Listen to as many Gilbert and Sullivan recordings as possible and pick your favourite tunes: we suggest 'O Leave Me Not' (*The Pirates Of Penzance*), 'The Sun and I' (*The Mikado*) or 'Take a Pair of Sparkling Eyes' (*The Gondoliers*). Add them to your repertoire.

Task 6

Write your own version of the 'Little List' patter song from *The Mikado*.

Task 7

Explore the nature and role of the various chorus groups in *The Pirates Of Penzance*. Why do you think that Gilbert was so strict and prescriptive in the original productions?

Task 8

Watch the movie *Topsy Turvy*. With whom do you sympathize most: Gilbert or Sullivan?

Task 9

Obviously, the modern successor of 'patter' is 'rap'. How do Stephen Sondheim (*Pacific Overtures* and *Into The Woods*) and Lin Miranda (*Hamilton*) use such musical forms and structures within the Musical format?

Stage four: Two more recent Musicals

Pacific Overtures

Teacher's notes

Following on from *The Mikado* by Gilbert and Sullivan, it would be appropriate to consider *Pacific Overtures* (1976), one of Stephen Sondheim's rather lesser-known Musicals, which he wrote with John Weidman. In exactly the same way that G & S took an historical figure and situation, this Musical considers the historical period of nineteenth-century Japan and the arrival of Commodore Matthew C. Perry, who attempted to move Japan out of isolation in order to create a more Westernised perspective. This was done through a form of 'gunboat diplomacy'.

Key facts

Pacific Overtures is a seminal work because it investigates some important historical facts regarding the relations between East and West through the Musical Theatre genre. It was clearly influential in the writing of the play *M. Butterfly* by David Henry Wang during the late 1980s. Sondheim and Weidman's Musical embraces the concept of 'ideas' rather than the composer and lyricist's usual 'character driven' work. Despite this the writing does control the narrative through the role of a samurai [Kayama]. Employing a clever device and the lyrics of his song 'A Bowler Hat', Kayama gradually changes during the course of the Musical, from a traditional Japanese warrior to adopting the characteristics of those he describes in the story. In the final moments of the Musical, Kayama becomes more like the people he oversees. The other character who offers a strong narrative element is the Americanized fisherman [Manjiro] who is familiar with life in the USA and sings the powerful musical number 'Four Black Dragons'.

Task 10

Ask your students to investigate the two key songs we have identified and prepare them for possible performance by a careful reading of the text and exploration of the context.

Key facts

The original production employed Japanese Kabuki and Noh theatrical conventions mixed with American Musical Theatre styles. The Musical had an all-male cast playing multiple roles –including females – except for the final moments, when 'more surprises next' predicates the arrival of at least twenty female actors for the last minutes (quite literally) of the final ensemble. The story is told through the lens of the Japanese. All aspects of the design were Japanese and the first production under the direction of Hal Prince was very stylized in presentation. Sondheim had to reconsider his composing style in order to create a score using a string of parallel 4ths that reflected the quasi-Japanese influences. Sondheim refers to this Musical as 'The most bizarre and unusual musical event to be seen in a commercial setting'.

Even though Sondheim's score evokes the Orient, at the beginning of Act Two of *Pacific Overtures* the musical number 'Please Hello' explores an essentially 'music hall' soundscape. First, we meet an American Admiral who brings messages from Commodore Perry and then we meet the British Admiral. The moment of our meeting the British Admiral Sondheim reflects the spirit of G & S as he sings/speaks in the form of a 'patter' song:

'Please Hello,
I come with letters from Her Majesty Victoria
Who, learning how you're trading now, sang "Hallelujah, Gloria!"

And sent me to convey to you her positive euphoria
As well as little gifts from Britain's various emporia.'

You might like to look at this YouTube link below:
https://www.youtube.com/watch?v=Z8WiudDlTBw

Hamilton

Teacher's notes

A natural trajectory from the political machinations of the USA in Japan is to travel back to the eighteenth century to discover the immigrant story of America where the character of Hamilton, a resourceful immigrant, arrives in America and is heard to say 'Hey, yo, I'm just like my country /I'm young scrappy and hungry'. The Musical **Hamilton** by Lin-Manuel Miranda explores the journey of this immigrant from his humble beginnings to becoming the first Treasury Secretary of the United States.

Key facts

In much the same way as Miranda mixes his history in the Musical *Hamilton* in order to make the narrative more compelling, so does the musical score reflect this same creative flair. Musical forms such as hip-hop, R&B, classical, operetta and Musical Theatre are all employed in the telling of Hamilton's story. The casting of the show reflects the mixed heritage of Alexander Hamilton and embraces opportunities to explore conscious multiracial, white and post-racial aspects of society.

In the operettas of G & S and the Musical Theatre of Sondheim, the 'patter' song is often used to explore and express the narrative. In the Musical *Hamilton* the 'patter' song is replaced by aspects of 'pop' culture such as 'rap' and 'hip-hop' and these musical structures are at the centre of the score. As a result, these musical devices push the narrative along at a pace that is 'driven' and exciting for the audience. The trick in performance is to identify the power of the consonant in the brisk articulative power of 'rap' and 'hip-hop' as opposed to the use of the vowel to express feelings.

The clear force of this Musical is its sense of urbanity. Following on from his previous Musical, *In The Heights*, Miranda shows how he can manipulate an audience to tap along to the music, enjoy the verbal and musical narrative and to be in collusion with the destiny of the characters.

Teacher's notes

It has suggested by some critics that Miranda has changed the face of the Musical by employing the music of 'pop' stations in order to attract a new kind of audience. We shall see, however, in our next lesson, that this claim could be made of Musicals from the late 1960s.

However, the clarity of the musical expression in *Hamilton* transcends time and its impact on audiences is that the ideas of yesterday can become the ideas of today. Miranda is more concerned with the narrative of each character rather than with the accuracy of historical and political 'facts'. The Musical attracts an audience who are looking for role models and for people to inspire them and offer leadership. An apparent disregard for the facts can be forgiven when other issues, such as life and how we deal with it, are considered.

Task 11

Now that you have introduced your students to the ideas of patter and rap in Musical Theatre we suggest that you set them the task of creating their own rap to the Pyramus and Thisbe performance scene from Shakespeare's *A Midsummer Night's Dream*. This well-known piece of Theatre has attracted many interpretations from performers as various as The Beatles to famous stand-up comics and never fails to capture the essence of interplay between performer and audience as in the opera 'A Midsummer Night's Dream' by Benjamin Britten.

A Musical Theatre exercise for a **rap** style musical:

Look at this short piece of text spoken by Quince as the Prologue from *A Midsummer Night's Dream* Act 5 scene (i) by William Shakespeare.

Now let your students experiment with the rhythm of the text and create the 'show' of **Pyramus and Thisbe** as a rap style musical theatre scene.

Gentles, perchance you wonder at this show;
But wonder on, till truth make all things plain.
This man is Pyramus, if you would know;

Set up a count of 4 to feel the beat. 1234 / 1234.
This will also prepare your students for speaking the text.

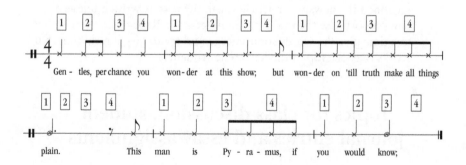

You can invent your own rhymes and ideas to tell a story. Create your own original RAP musical theatre number as below:

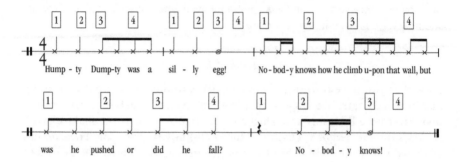

Further tasks

Ask your students to:

1 Create an original piece of Musical Theatre by fusing either two different styles of dance or music together. Devise a scenario for this number and choose a 'pop' song and by using the lyrics, change the drive and energy of the song by adopting a 'rap' style over the harmonic sequence of the song.

2 Listen to a selection of rap artists including Eminem and Tupac. Try to work out how they deliver the words and engage with the music underscoring their lyrics. Using the words and score aim to create a Musical Theatre scene using the context of the song to support the action, physicality and setting.

3 Find an appropriate newspaper article that has dramatic content. Choose a repeated chord sequence such as: I – VI - IV – V - IV/V – I or the well-known ground bass Purcell's 'Dido's Lament'. Having identified the newspaper article speak the text as written but as a news report. Use the music as an underscore. Repeat the exercise but this time give the words some energy and try to give it a rhythm that works over the top of the harmonic sequence.

Topics for class discussion, student journal entries and essay assignments

1 In her poem 'Spelling' Margaret Atwood writes ". . . words and words and words and power". Looking at the Musical *Hamilton* do you think this description might apply to the score?

2 Sondheim commented on the musical score of *Hamilton* as being 'fresh and meticulous and theatrical'. Do you agree?

3 Can you suggest why the Musical *Hamilton* was more of a commercial success than *Pacific Overtures*?

4 The opening musical number of *Pacific Overtures* is recognized as being a significant moment in the history of the Musical. Can you think of any other opening numbers that have such dramatic importance and suggest reasons why? You might like to consider the Musicals: *Oklahoma!*; *On the Town*; *'Falsetto'*; *Kiss Me Kate*; *A Chorus Line*; *Sweeney Todd*; *Fame* and *Pippin*.

5 Discuss the quality of dance within *Pacific Overtures*.

6 Introducing the cast of *Hamilton* at the Tony Awards, 12 June 2016, Michelle Obama suggested that America was 'a place of opportunity, where no matter how humble our origins we can make it if we try.' Do you think the Musical *Hamilton* supports this statement?

7 Consider the musical number 'My Shot', where the character Hamilton introduces himself with a dramatic rhythmic rap to show off both verbal and political dexterity. How does this scene clarify 'The American Dream'?

8 The musical number 'The Room Where it Happens' identifies major decisions about the nation's future as characters talk together in a room. Identify how successful this number is in illustrating the nature of power.

9 *The Beggar's Opera* of 1728 contained many references to political and real-life situations. *Hamilton*, written 287 years later, tells the story of a man who really existed but amidst a set of fictional and theatrical events! What similarities can you discover about these two Musicals in both the treatment of the narrative and score?

10 Look at the use of 'popular' song and how each Musical uses the score to support the narrative.

11 Compare the treatment of the characters Macheath and Hamilton.

12 *Holler If Ya Hear Me*, a jukebox Musical crafted from the music of late rapper Tupac Shakur, had its debut on Broadway in 2013, but was not a success. Try to discover as much as you can about this Musical.

13 Some Musicals which investigate historical figures are listed below:

Rodgers & Hart	*Dearest Enemy*	1925
Bock & Harnick	*Fiorello!*	1959
Bock & Harnick	*The Rothschilds*	1970
Bernstein & Lerner	*1600 Pennsylvania Avenue*	1976

Lloyd Webber & Tim Rice	*Evita*	1979
Sondheim & Weidman	*Assassins*	1990
Jason Robert Brown	*Parade*	1998

Look at two of these Musicals and compare and contrast the treatment of the central figures and how the ideas are expressed in each Musical.

Miranda suggests that rap is 'uniquely suited to tell Hamilton's story because it has more words per measure than any other musical genre.' Why is this use of 'rap' so important and what is its impact in the telling of the story?

SAMPLE TEST QUESTIONS
(MULTIPLE CHOICE)

1 The works of Gilbert and Sullivan first became popular in:
a) The United States b) Victorian England c) Paris d) The last century.

2 *The Mikado* is set in: a) New York b) Ireland c) Japan d) China.

3 Songs in which as many words as possible are spoken/sung are known as: a) Rap b) Verse c) Jokes d) Patter.

4 *Pacific Overtures* has a score and lyrics by: a) Gilbert and Sullivan b) Sondheim c) Miranda d) Rodgers and Hart.

5 *The Mikado*, *Pacific Overtures* and *M. Butterfly* have in common that they: a) Deal with the topic of war b) Are full of patter c) Are set in Japan d) Discuss politics.

6 *Hamilton* uses: a) An all-white chorus b) A chorus of women c) An all-black cast d) A chorus of cotton pickers.

7 One of the most obvious features of *Hamilton* is that it draws upon: a) Myths b) Popular dance and music forms c) Patriotism d) Famous choreographers.

8 The character of Hamilton reflects aspects of: a) Gang violence b) Prejudice c) Showbiz d) The American Dream.

9 Gilbert and Sullivan pioneered: a) A far more disciplined use of the chorus b) Rock music c) Serious issues in the Theatre d) The use of humour.

10 Sondheim had in common with Gilbert and Sullivan that he: a) Used popular dance forms b) Drew upon historical events and characters c) Wrote only the music or lyrics d) Was experimental in the form of his Theatre writing.

Reflection: Lesson Nine

You may have found it challenging to introduce students to the work of Gilbert and Sullivan, especially if you were not previously familiar with them yourself.

After your experience in this lesson what were the features, melodies or scenes which you found to be most attractive or appealing to your students? How might you introduce them differently on a future occasion? We have frequently referred to the fact that learning invariably involves making connections and this lesson deliberately sets out to facilitate that. Common strands such as 'patter' leading to 'rap' or a fictional Japan linking with *Pacific Overtures* should enable students to progress in their understanding and realize the relevance of exploring the unfamiliar. How successful were you in exploiting these connections?

Whereas the works of Gilbert and Sullivan may seem remote and almost irrelevant, *Hamilton* has become almost an icon for our times. Think about the reasons for this as you plan future work. Why, for instance, did a highly intelligent and inventive director like Miller take the trouble to recreate *The Mikado* for the modern stage? What qualities does this work possess to make such a project worthwhile? Which other operettas by Gilbert and Sullivan would you wish to give what Miller liked to term an 'afterlife'?

We have made frequent reference to Stephen Sondheim in this book for very obvious reasons: he is an almost unique creative artist in the modern Theatre, but why is his *Pacific Overtures* not better known? Keep this question in mind because we shall be continuing to press you to explore the lesser known and sometimes almost totally unknown works as a means of providing a rich learning experience for your students.

Think back now to the experience of discussing and finding extracts from *Hamilton*. To what extent does this work promote black performers and performance modes? Can it operate outside of a powerful cultural tradition or can other Musicals now be adapted to draw on other ethnic traditions? If you were to work on a production of *Hamilton*, which students in your class might provide the expertise in language, singing or dance that would be needed? Might you need to draw on the help of other colleagues? Conversely, how might a predominantly black cast react to staging Gilbert and Sullivan?

We suggest that, before you embark on subsequent lessons, you quickly survey the topics we have suggested for the future. Identify some of the works we shall be introducing and decide how you can ensure that topics and themes you have already discussed and worked with can be developed in conjunction with what we are proposing. Consider also how you might continue to reflect the ethnic and gender diversity of your class in your approach and look for additional material which might enable you to ensure total inclusivity in your work.

The operettas of Gilbert and Sullivan became immensely popular with community and amateur companies largely because they were relatively accessible and frequently amusing. You might reflect on the possibility that we have lost something valuable in their neglect!

Lesson Ten

Book, Music and Lyrics

Lesson themes

Students often fail to realize the importance of knowing and acknowledging the names of the writers of their favourite Musicals or songs. This is not only profoundly depressing but shows a lack of interest, context and courtesy. We outline all the major contributors to the writing of a show and introduce the correct terminology to employ when creating a programme. By way of example we introduce students to the work of two remarkable creators of Musical Theatre works from different periods and places: Ivor Novello from London's 'West End' and Stephen Sondheim from New York's 'Broadway'.

Teaching objectives

- To establish the importance of making correct acknowledgement of works
- To explain the various roles and aspects of creating a work of Musical Theatre
- To introduce students to two remarkable figures from Musical Theatre history and to enhance their sense of context
- To further explore themes from earlier lessons that emerge in the works to be studied
- To enable students to develop writing and/or performance skills based on their understanding.

Key facts, teacher's notes and in-class activities for students

Stage one: Establishing the basics

Every Musical tells a story: without a story there is no drama and no interest. Some Musicals, like *Oklahoma!* or *My Fair Lady*, are based on pre-existing plays and others, like *Les Misérables* are based on books. Some writers prefer to write their own stories but however the Musical takes shape, it will culminate in a '**book**', which is the technical name we give to the printed dialogue and stage directions. When the **book** also contains the words of the songs, which are known as **lyrics**, it becomes **the libretto**. Usually, but not always, the **book** and **lyrics** are written by the same person. In some Musicals the dialogue and lyrics are all sung: in which case we describe the show as **sung through,** but it is quite common for a show to contain spoken dialogue and songs of various kinds.

Usually, the music will be written by someone else in close co-operation with the **Dramatist** (writer of the book and lyrics) but there have been some famous exceptions and it is fascinating to learn of two remarkable people who not only wrote the book, lyrics and music but, in one case also took the leading role in the stage production of the shows he had created.

Stage two: Exploring a remarkable example

Teacher's notes

As a teacher you may not have been aware of the work of the Welsh actor, dramatist and composer Ivor Novello (1893–1951) and it is quite possible that your students may never have heard of him: this, in fact, makes the act of rediscovery all the more exciting. Novello holds a record for being the author, composer and leading actor for four successive Musical Comedies (or Musicals as we now call them) in London's West End from 1935–45: we cannot afford to ignore such talent in our exploration of this art form!

Key facts

Ivor Novello first came to prominence with a patriotic song he wrote during the First World War: 'Keep the Home Fires Burning'. This song, alone, is worth exploring as an exercise in inspiring melody and words which exactly captured the *zeitgeist* of the period in which it was written. Novello's parents tried to discourage him from making a career of the stage but his ambition prevailed.

Novello continued to respond to the spirit of the age during the latter half of the 'Great Depression' in Britain. His ability to capture a romantic sense of escapism and glamour provided a much-needed tonic to audiences who had grown tired of imported 'revues' and other trivial stage works that had come to dominate the London stage.

Novello's first major success was his Musical Comedy *Glamorous Nights*, which opened at London's Theatre Royal in Drury Lane in 1935. For this show, Ivor Novello wrote both the book and the music but invited the poet Christopher Hassall to write the lyrics. Novello himself took the leading role! The show was described as 'a romantic story of opera, revolution, and intrigue in the modern Ruritanian state of "Krasnia".' We see here already that Novello is writing about the Theatre (remember Lesson Seven) and gives his story a romantic setting in an imaginary State with rather exciting implications. He also established a tradition that he would take the leading role and it is highly likely that he wrote the 'book' with that in mind.

Task 1

Research Novello's previous career as an actor. What can you discover about his acting of Shakespeare and on film?

Key facts

Novello's two subsequent Musical Comedies, both produced at Drury Lane, followed a similar pattern: *Careless Rapture* (1936) and *Crest of the Wave* (1937) both had lyrics by Christopher Hassall whilst the other major aspects of the work were created by Ivor Novello, who also played the leading role. Once again, Novello explored an aspect of 'Showbusiness'. *Crest of the Wave* was described as 'An extravaganza set in Hollywood about the escapades, connivances and loves of a group of actors, producers and directors'. So, as ominous political storm clouds were gathering over Europe, Novello took his audiences on an escapist and romantic journey away from depression and reality.

Task 2

Read the following tribute written by a Theatre historian after Novello's death in 1951. What impression do you form of his life and how does it relate to your ambitions and outlook?

> He was the complete man of the Theatre. He had no life outside it at all. In the brief periods when he was not actually in his dressing room or on the stage, he was surrounded by Theatre folk, he talked Theatre, he thought and he dreamt Theatre. No wonder he understood his calling, for to those who really love it, the Theatre must be a full-time job. So it was with Ivor.
>
> W. MACQUEEN-POPE

Do you agree with the ideas expressed here? Does this explain why Novello frequently chose to write about Showbusiness?

Key facts

Ivor Novello's next major success, *The Dancing Years* (1939) opened shortly before the outbreak of the Second World War and, after a brief opening run at Drury Lane, went out on tour because, with the onset of war, London theatres were closed. Once again, Novello relied on the playwright and poet Christopher Hassall to provide the lyrics but he created the book, music and leading acting role himself. This production explored one of the themes of an earlier lesson in this book: 'Programs in the East'. It followed the career of a Jewish composer from Vienna who has a love affair with his leading singer but risks the fate of many such Jewish creatives in a Nazi-controlled world. We have already seen how musicians from Vienna and other European centres of Musical Theatre were forced to flee, often to the safety of New York, where they became leading figures in the establishment of Musical Theatre on Broadway.

The Dancing Years remained one of Novello's most popular works and was made into a film in 1950 and an Ice Show in 1954.

Task 3

Find recordings of videos of *The Dancing Years* and identify some of its most popular songs. Why do you think that the dancing aspect of this story was so important to contemporary audiences in the years during and after the war?

Key facts

Ivor Novello's first post-war work was *Perchance to Dream* and was produced at the huge Hippodrome Theatre in London in April 1945. This marked yet another stage in the creator's development because he elected to write not only the book and music but also the lyrics. The results were remarkable and he provided songs of enduring popularity that prompted critics to liken Novello to Gilbert and Sullivan with their ability to craft songs that would remain favourites of English-speaking performers and audiences throughout the world.

With *King's Rhapsody* (Palace Theatre 1949) Novello returned to using Hassall as his librettist and to his passion for writing about imaginary lands, in this case 'Murania'. For the last time, he kept the lead role for himself and, as he had always done, surrounded himself with some of the most popular actors of the day from stage and screen.

Task 4

Ask your students to research the careers of Novello's leading actors. What qualities did these particular performers bring to their roles and why were they chosen?

Key facts

Ivor Novello did not act in his final successful production *Gay's The Word* and, although he wrote the book and music, he employed the writer Alan Melville to write the lyrics. Significantly, however, he once again set his work in the Theatre: in this case in the modern Theatre where an 'old trouper' is attempting to establish a drama school. To some extent, therefore, he was pioneering the creation of 'performing arts school' dramas that were to become so popular in film and television at a later stage.

Ironically, the title of the piece, *Gay's The Word*, does not refer to Novello's or any of his characters' sexuality even though he was, in fact, part of the extensive but repressed and secretive gay scene of the Theatre of his time. This was, of course, a problem with which he had to struggle. Ivor Novello died whilst he was still performing in *King's Rhapsody* and in discussion with the impresario Tom Arnold about a possible new Musical about a Russian Count set in Edwardian times. His main lyricist, Christopher Hassall, gave a memorial address at a service in his memory in which he explained that Novello reacted to the 'forlorn' nature of the age 'subjected to unparalleled stresses' by taking people to another land: a land of 'might have been'.

Stage three: Working with examples

Teacher's notes

By far the best way to introduce students to the work of Novello is to let them sing some of his best songs. If you have already introduced them to 'Keep the Home Fires Burning' (a song that has more recently been incorporated into a Theatre piece about the First World War by the composer David Burridge, whose work we shall encounter later) then move on to 'We'll Gather Lilacs' or 'Love is my Reason' from *Perchance to Dream*. Have your students research the storyline and context of these songs and ask them to explain the title of the show.

Task 5

Ask your students to respond to the following questions and assignments:

1   What were the fashions, including hairstyles, being worn by characters in the original productions of Ivor Novello's shows?

2 Look for illustrations of the first productions: why do you think Novello acquired 'star' status?

3 Find extracts containing a song and work on a small performance of that incident.

Stage four: A more recent example to introduce

Teacher's notes

Another fascinating example of a multitalented practitioner is the American Stephen Sondheim and introducing his work to students is always a stimulating activity. They will probably have encountered his lyrics to *West Side Story* (1957) but not be aware that he went on to write the lyrics and the music for a whole string of Broadway successes. Unlike Novello, he never wrote the book for any show and did not act in them, but the great director Trevor Nunn, who created *Cats*, considered him as gifted as Shakespeare or Chekhov as a writer.

Key facts

Stephen Sondheim was born in New York in 1930 when Ivor Novello was about to enter his most productive period of writing. Like so many of the Jewish men and women in the USA who were to play a prominent part in the Theatre, Sondheim traced his family origins to Europe (see Lesson 6). He fell in love with the Theatre at the age of nine and, at the time of writing, he continues to create work at the age of ninety. Unlike Novello, Sondheim was able to benefit from the much more progressive attitudes to the arts in colleges in the USA and he studied Theatre and Literature before going on to graduate school to study musical composition.

A defining moment in Sondheim's life was his meeting as a young man with the librettist Oscar Hammerstein II, who agreed to mentor him. As a result, Sondheim developed into one of the most gifted lyricists of all time. His contribution to *West Side Story* was a major contributory factor to a show which, with its story of gang violence, racial tension and prejudice and poor relations with the police, seems as relevant today as ever. This was to become typical of Sondheim who, rather than escaping into romanticism, preferred to confront aspects of life head-on. Many of his Musicals were to be unconventional and experimental and were not always particularly popular or successful, but they all repay careful investigation. The song 'Send in the Clowns' from *A Little Night Music* (1973) has remained one of Sondheim's best-known songs and has had more than 500 commercial recordings.

Fortunately for us Sondheim has provided a rich primary source for understanding his approach to the writing of lyrics in his book *Finishing The Hat* (2010) and we would strongly recommend frequent reference to this work.

Stage five: Exploring Sondheim's work and approach

Task 6

1   Students will enjoy singing along to a recording of or your keyboard accompaniment to 'Tonight', 'Maria' or 'America' from *West Side Story* initially; let them savour the lyrics: notice particularly: a) the use of repetition b) the very varied rhythms c) the use of rhyme.

2   Now let them find another song from the show that involves at least two voices. Notice how Sondheim is developing his skill whilst using the glorious music of Leonard Bernstein.

3   Divide the class into two and assign each half one of the roles in the song 'Make of our Lives, One Life'. Notice the way in which this is really sung dialogue as if the characters were taking part in a wedding ceremony. In pairs speak the words as sincere dialogue **before** making any attempt at singing. If possible, re-enact the scene using the music.

Task 7

Ask your students to find examples of the following statements by Sondheim in *Finishing The Hat*:

1   'for what are solo songs but musicalized soliloquies.' (pxxi)

2   '(the song) loses much of its tone and all of its subtext when disconnected from the placid surface of its music.' (p.xxi)

3   'In song, music is an equal partner.' (p.xix)

4   'Content dictates form.' (p.xv)

Key facts

Sondheim's first work for which he wrote both the music and lyrics was *Saturday Night* (1954), which he described as a 'Musical Comedy'. The book was by Julius J. Epstein (another Jewish writer) and this was based on a play: *Front Porch In Flatbush* by Julius J. and Philip J. Epstein. This genesis of a work of Musical Theatre was typical of that of many Broadway shows and, with his knowledge of Ancient Greece and its drama, Sondheim went on at a later stage to provide the music and lyrics for *A Funny Thing Happened On The Way To The Forum* (1962) and *The Frogs* (1974), which was based on the play by Aristophanes and went on to have a memorable production in a swimming pool in the UK!

Further successful productions included *Company* (1970), which explored relationships and inner lives in an experimentally 'plotless' structure and

Follies (1971): Sondheim's contribution to a growing number of shows set in the life of the Theatre (see Lesson 7) and *Sweeney Todd, The Demon Barber Of Fleet Street* (1979): a horror story set in nineteenth-century London. His *Merrily We Roll Along* (1981) and *Into The Woods* (2014), based on fairy tales by the Brothers Grimm and Charles Perrault, both continued to push the boundaries of what is possible in a Musical.

Task 8

The internet offers very substantial amounts of information about Stephen Sondheim, who seems to have worked with all the major figures in the development of Musical Theatre in the twentieth and twenty-first centuries. Ask your students to go online and discover all they can about his partnerships and lesser-known works. Then:

Select a Musical with music and lyrics by Sondheim that has been staged by student Theatre or off-Broadway/fringe companies and try out scenes for yourselves.

Stage six: Learning from Sondheim

Task 9

When Sondheim first met Oscar Hammerstein II and sought his help in writing for the Theatre, the famous librettist set the young man the following tasks: we recommend that you find a way in which you can challenge your students with the same task:

1   Adapt a good play as a Musical.
2   Adapt a flawed play as a Musical.
3   Adapt another form such as a novel or short story into a Musical.
4   Write a Musical entirely from your own devising.

Task 10

Ask your students to recall the tasks they undertook in Lessons Two and Three and review their efforts in the light of the following comments in the Preface of Sondheim's book *Finishing the Hat*:

*   Content dictates form
*   Less is more
*   God is in the details
*   All in the service of:
*   Clarity (p.xv)

Topics for class discussion, student journal entries or essay assignments

1 Why do you think that Ivor Novello wrote in a romantic vein?

2 What would be the challenges of taking the lead role in your own work?

3 How do the Musicals of Novello and Sondheim differ?

4 Explore the structure and then the effect of Sondheim's lyrics in *West Side Story*.

5 Discover the shows with both music and lyrics written by Sondheim between 1959 and 1981. How many of these shows became well-known?

6 Why do you think Sondheim decided to write his own music but never wrote his own book?

7 Research some of the writers of the books of Sondheim's best-known Musicals. How did Sondheim adapt these for the stage?

8 Notice how Sondheim is another example of the Jewish background of writers for the Musical Theatre: what can you discover about his European Jewish origins? (See Lesson Six.)

9 The Theatre historian, Kurt Ganzl (1995) wrote: 'Sondheim followed his outstanding show (*A Little Night Music*) with an idiosyncratic set of Musicals that won an idiosyncratic following.' Do you agree?

SAMPLE TEST QUESTIONS (MULTIPLE CHOICE)

1 Ivor Novello was writing: a) In the jazz age b) In the period of the Great Depression c) In the Edwardian period d) During the French Revolution.

2 Novello's work was largely: a) Fatalistic b) Satirical c) Romantic d) Stylized.

3 The song 'We'll Gather Lilacs' comes from: a) *King's Rhapsody* b) *South Pacific* c) *Perchance to Dream* d) *Evita*.

4 Novello wrote a Musical that tells of a Jewish composer from: a) Vienna b) New York c) Jerusalem d) London.

5 Stephen Sondheim differed from Novello in that: a) He never acted in one of his major shows b) He did not write the 'book' for his

Musicals c) He had successes on Broadway and in the West End d) All of these.

6 The title *A Little Night Music* by Sondheim is an ironic quotation from the name of a Musical work by: a) Handel b) Bernstein c) Mozart d) Andrew Lloyd Webber.

7 *Into the Woods* is based on: a) A novel b) An existing play c) A movie d) Fairy tales.

8 Sondheim and Novello explored the life of Showbusiness in their show: a) *Follies* b) *Sweeney Todd* c) *Crest Of The Wave* d) *The Dancing Years*.

9 Sondheim's works were very different from Novello's because they: a) Told a story b) Were sometimes experimental in form c) Included memorable songs d) Achieved long runs in the Theatre.

10 Sondheim considered that the essential quality of lyric writing was: a) Rhythm b) Clarity c) Rhyme d) Humour.

Reflection: Lesson Ten

In this chapter we singled out two major contributors to the ever-changing world of Musical Theatre. Your students will probably be more familiar with the more recent musicals of Jason Robert Brown or Andrew Lloyd Webber or the 'Mega' Musicals *Les Misérables* and *Miss Saigon*. Musicals such as *Kinky Boots*, *Dear Evan Hansen*, *Spring Awakening* and *Hamilton* will also feature in their listening and viewing lists.

All these Musicals have something significant to offer the audience as they each approach the narrative from a different perspective. Like those of Novello and Sondheim, some Musicals are based on the book, a historical period, a fairy tale or a moment of creative imagination. It would be useful for you and your students to consider at least ten contemporary Musicals and define the style and type of narrative and how they might differ from each other. As a follow-up to this lesson collect a series of **YouTube** versions to support your discoveries and download these for future reference.

A useful development of the investigation undertaken in this lesson would be to encourage the critical thinking of your students as audience members, so prepare a 'viewing list' for them to use:

1 Choose, discuss and compare TWO contemporary composers of Musicals from the USA and UK, such as Jason Robert Brown, Lin-Manuel Miranda (USA) or Andrew Lloyd Webber (UK).

2 Identify how these composers and lyricists (where appropriate) approach the narrative and structure of each Musical.

3   Explore the structure and form of each Musical chosen and consider
    the influence that each individual Musical number has on the
    narrative.

4   It is always interesting to discover how a Musical begins (overture)
    and ends (finale) and how it attracts its audience to focus on the
    narrative and understand the dramatic situation. Did your students
    recognize the qualities in the opening of a Musical and how it
    influences the narrative as it unfolds? What was the lasting
    impression of the overture? What was the power and impact of the
    opening section of the Musical?

Set your students to investigate how important the opening number is and
what they notice in terms of plot, narrative and establishment of character.
Does the audience meet everyone at the start of the Musical or do they get
to meet them as the Musical develops?

As you and your students reflect on the varied qualities of Musicals in
this comparative approach, take your thoughts further to ask how each
Musical differs in letting the characters identify their dramatic purpose in
the action. How does each Musical number indicate these desires? How
many of these musical numbers are there in each Musical? What does each
musical number achieve in terms of the narrative? Can you recognize the
different styles of musical number within each Musical: ballads, narrative,
legit, character, pop/rock number, rap, patter, eleven o'clock numbers, and
an 'I want' number?

Lesson Eleven

Rebellion and Censorship

Lesson themes

As we have seen from the previous lessons, there has been a constant flow of works of Musical Theatre across the Atlantic ever since New York became a major centre of creativity in the early years of the twentieth century. However, the 1960s became a pivotal time for the creation of the Musical as a commodity which can be marketed and exported. This development was brought about by the abolition of Theatre censorship in the UK as well as by significant changes in the political and artistic movements in the US. Students need to understand these issues which have shaped our modern creative industry.

Teaching objectives

- To give students an understanding of the contextual and historical issues which have created the modern Musical
- To explain and investigate the influence of the abolition of censorship in the British Theatre and the dominance of both Broadway and the West End
- To explore the links between social issues and the Musical
- To develop an understanding of the interaction between the rock/ pop industry and the Musical and of a new kind of audience.

Key facts, teacher's notes and in-class activities for students

Stage one: Investigating the 'spirit of an age'

Teacher's notes

We must always remember that it is our job as teachers to help our students to **make connections** in order to enhance their knowledge and understanding. The events explored in the lesson will probably seem like ancient history to your students and possibly to you, but an ability to see the relevance of events from the past, and particularly, the growth of what is sometimes termed 'youth culture', will expand the horizons and enrich the whole experience of exploring Musical Theatre.

Key facts

Here are some of the key events and developments you might introduce through video clips, recordings and live communal singing:

1   In the 1960s the USA is embroiled in a war in Vietnam and there is increasing opposition to this use of force, particularly from a younger, student generation. There are many 'on-campus' protests.

2   Disillusionment with the principles and attitudes of the older generation leads to a growth of 'hippie' culture, preferring love and peace to hatred, war and out-moded ideas of order.

3   Rock music becomes a major channel for the expression of rebellion.

4   In the US the new 'tribal rock Musical' *Hair* encapsulates these ideas.

5   In 1968 in the UK, after centuries of state censorship of the Theatre, the office of the official censor is abolished.

6   Prior to that moment the censor (the Lord Chamberlain) has forbidden: a) representation of God or Christ on stage b) nudity on stage c) obscene or blasphemous language on stage.

Stage two: Reflection

Now is the moment to make connections!
Consider these events:

1   *Hair* contains an optional nude scene: once censorship is abolished the show transfers to London.

2   *Godspell* and *Jesus Christ Superstar*, both of which tell aspects of the life of Jesus, become enormously popular in spite of protests

from some Christian groups. Both shows are seen on either side of the Atlantic. *Superstar* becomes the first in a line of remarkable shows with music by Andrew Lloyd Webber and book and lyrics by Tim Rice to dominate both the West End and Broadway and eventually to be 'packaged' to be seen in almost every major city in the world.

3 *Jesus Christ Superstar* opens on Broadway in 1971 but is preceded by the release of the album, which achieves 'hit' status before anyone is able to see the live show. In both *Superstar* and *Godspell* the lead role is played by well-known pop/rock singers.

4 The TV show 'Fame' builds on the idea that Musical Theatre, with its blend of dance, drama and singing, is a desirable career for young people to inhabit.

Stage three: Practical exploration

Tasks

1 Teach the entire class some of the following songs and explore what qualities they seem to have in common: 'Let the Sunshine in' or 'The Age of Aquarius' from *Hair*, 'Day by Day' from *Godspell*, 'Fame: I Want to Live for Ever' from *Fame*. Supply the names of the writers of the music, book and lyrics for these three shows.

2 In groups, create choreography for each song.

3 In groups, improvise the telling of one of the parables of Jesus: for example 'The Prodigal Son', 'The Sower', 'The Good Samaritan'. Compare the results with the stories told in *Godspell*.

4 Listen to the songs sung by Mary Magdalene in *Jesus Christ Superstar*, then work on scenes in which other characters interact with her.

Stage four: The cultural context

Key facts

The Theatre producer and music journalist Tony Jasper (2010) points out that it was actually 'Stephen Sondheim's *Company* which broke the traditional score mould established by such people as Rodgers & Hammerstein' (p.80). In Sondheim's Musical we are taken into the 'realism of life' and shown the upper-middle class who are 'spiritually empty' (ibid.). In this world, says the New York publication *Village Voice*, 'no one dreams, only survives' (ibid.).

Company established a kind of Musical in which the entire cast is on stage throughout the performance as if engaged in some form of mutual celebration. In contrast to the spiritual emptiness of the characters in *Company*, the Musical *Hair* was, in Jasper's words: 'an enticing mix of profane language, nudity, sexual stimulation and a disregard for the very moral fabric of society' (80). It also moved easily from hallucinatory drugs to quotations from the Christian service of Holy Communion. *Hair* reflected not only the interests of a generation that listened to The Rolling Stones and Led Zeppelin, but also sought out spiritual nourishment with an interest in Eastern religions and the huge 'Inner Peace Movement'. Aspects of the work, with its sense of freedom, were also embraced by the Women's Liberation Movement.

Tim Rice and Andrew Lloyd Webber had already enjoyed considerable success with their rock/pop 'Cantata' *Joseph And The Amazing Technicolor Dreamcoat* prior to their creating *Superstar*. This genre had become increasingly popular in schools and with youth choirs and churches. It seemed that nothing was now too sacred to form the basis of a Musical. Accordingly, the rock and religious-based Musicals not only attracted a new, young audience, but the attention of the Musical and religious press. Fascination with these shows extended to the wider media and provoked comments from journalists, prominent church figures and campaigners of many kinds.

The story of the genesis of *Jesus Christ Superstar*, which was to become the longest-running Musical in London's West End at that time, is told in Lloyd Webber's autobiography *Unmasked* (2018). The son of a composer of church music and devotee of Elvis and Opera, Lloyd Webber was eventually to work with a number of librettists. But, with Tim Rice he created a succession of Musicals that would reverse the transatlantic trend which had dominated the Theatre for many years. From the early 1970s onwards, British Musicals, cleverly marketed and packaged, came to conquer both the West End and Broadway and were seen in major cities throughout the English-speaking world and beyond.

Tasks

1   Ask your students to find press reviews of the original productions of the Musicals we have been discussing in this lesson: what do they reveal about the impact these shows had in their time?

2   Explore the score of *Joseph And The Amazing Technicolor Dreamcoat* and sing some of the songs collectively. Help your students to recognize what forms of music are being parodied: e.g. a French Cabaret song 'Those Canaan Days' or a heavy 'Elvis' number, 'I Was Walking Along'.

3 Ask your students to discover the other librettists who have contributed to the work of Andrew Lloyd Webber.

4 Explore the short work *Tell Me On A Sunday* by Andrew Lloyd Webber and Don Black. This Musical for a single performer might form the basis of a similar work for students to create for themselves.

5 Work with your students on possible movement qualities for the characters in Lloyd Webber's *Cats* based on the poems of T. S. Eliot. Ask them to work in pairs in creating convincing cats and compare the results with the various songs in the Musical.

Topics for class discussion, student journal entries or essay assignments

1 Why do you think there were protests against shows portraying aspects of the life of Jesus on stage?

2 Why was the war in Vietnam so divisive in American Society?

3 What is your understanding of 'hippie' culture and what effect did it have on music and Theatre?

4 Why are the works you have been exploring often known as 'Rock Musicals' or 'Rock Operas'? How did they differ in form and style from previous Musicals?

5 *West Side Story* is often cited as the first Musical to embrace the ideas of a distinctive 'youth culture'. How do the shows we have been discussing here extend that idea?

6 How has Andrew Lloyd Webber's production company created visual and performance images that have enabled his Musicals to be seen in similar form throughout the world? Name four of his most popular shows: who wrote the book and lyrics?

SAMPLE TEST QUESTIONS
(MULTIPLE CHOICE)

1 *Hair* was able to transfer to London because of: a) A change in attitudes b) A protest movement c) The abolition of censorship d) Economic factors.

2 Some thinkers consider that a new kind of Musical was established by: a) *My Fair Lady* b) *Company* c) *Cabaret* d) *The Sound of Music*.

3 The leading roles in early productions of *Godspell* and *Jesus Christ Superstar* were played by: a) Teenagers b) Established actors c) Rock/pop stars d) Unknowns.

4 Censorship in the UK Theatre was abolished in: a) 1968 b) 1930 c) 1971 d) 1920.

5 *Hair* and *Jesus Christ Superstar* attracted the attention of:
a) Conventional critics b) The music press c) Television d) Politicians.

6 The success of Andrew Lloyd Webber and Tim Rice's Musicals was greatly enhanced by: a) The critical reaction b) The set design c) Releasing the album prior to the production d) The choreography.

7 *Hair* resonated with an audience already interested in: a) Inner peace b) Communism c) Socialism d) Global warming.

8 *Godspell* is based on: a) The Koran b) The Parables of Jesus c) The death of Christ d) The Last Supper.

9 *Godspell* is the old Anglo-Saxon word for 'Gospel' and means:
a) A spell cast by God b) Good news c) Help d) God's love.

10 *Hair* was seen as a protest against: a) Communism b) Christianity c) The war in Vietnam d) Censorship in the British Theatre.

Reflection: Lesson Eleven

This lesson may have raised some challenging questions because there has been a considerable shift in political and faith issues since the events with which we have been dealing.

For example, a recent BBC television programme repeated a popular song and dance show from the 1970s which included a complete choreographed re-enactment of the life and death of Jesus. It is difficult to imagine such an item being shown today as a form of popular entertainment. You may well have found that your students were either indifferent to or puzzled by the reactions of Christian groups to such Musicals as *Godspell* or, because they are of other faiths or none, were totally ignorant of the events being put on stage. They may have been equally unaware of the student passions that ran so high during the war in Vietnam or the cultural current that was running through the campuses of the 1960s.

How were you able to bridge these generational and cultural gulfs? How did the ethnic and gender diversity of your group of students affect their perceptions of what, for them, were distant events?

Students, ideally, will emerge from this lesson with a clearer perception of the transatlantic nature of the Musical and its relatively recent dependence on the recording industry. Reflect, also, on the extent to which Musicals are made popular and accessible through film and other visual media and how this constantly impacts on new generations of students. They can now summon up almost any item of Musical Theatre they wish and compare their own performances with those of the most experienced and sophisticated of performers: what is the effect of this, particularly on their own originality?

Reflect also on the fact that it is possible to see an almost identical production of one of the currently most popular Musicals in a huge range of cities and towns throughout the world. The 'packaging' of Musicals in this way was largely developed by the organizations supporting the works co-created by Andrew Lloyd Webber. What is the effect of this phenomenon on the aspirations and interests of current students and how does this relate to the indigenous cultures of the countries to which Musicals are now exported? Is it, perhaps, time to create Musicals which tell stories from a wider world, using performance modes from non-Western cultures?

As you come to teach using the final lesson in this book, you will be invited to explore material drawn from lesser-known but equally gifted writers who have chosen to use the Musical to celebrate local issues and alternative forms of Theatre. What are the topics which now engage your students as opposed to those which drove the 1960s and 70s? How can we harness the passions, talents and interests of our generation to create Musicals which will resonate with new audiences?

In addition to performance skills, what are the critical, technical and promotional skills that will ensure the future health of this industry?

Lesson Twelve

The Burning of the Boats – The Musical Is Alive and Well

Lesson themes

Students and teachers often confine themselves to using and learning about Musicals which have become well-known through their success in the commercial Theatre and/or on film. The results are often little more than an attempt to recreate the glamour of the original performance and to imitate the various forms of recording that become available. However, a glance at the listings of Theatre activity in major towns and cities will reveal that not only are the majority of productions Musicals, but that 'fringe', 'off-Broadway' and community productions are increasingly exploring new, original and fascinating Musicals which may never reach conventional universal recognition. Such works are often the life-blood of Theatre if it is to survive and reward exploration and serious consideration. The creation of new and original work is the main theme of this lesson.

Teaching objectives

- To make students aware of the broadest possible concept of Musical Theatre
- To inspire students to create their own work for the Theatre
- To provide insights into the creation of a new Musical
- To encourage critical thinking about Musical Theatre
- To help students understand more fully the roles of writer and composer.

Key facts, teacher's notes and in-class activities for students

Stage one: Widening horizons

Task 1

Ask your students to read the following Theatre review of a new Musical very carefully and comment on it. It is likely that neither you nor they will ever have heard of this work but (and this is an important learning point), that does not mean that it is of any lesser quality than some which may become widely known. Use the simple test of asking them 'what do you now know about this Musical that you did not know when you came into class today?':

The Burning of the Boats

A Musical Theatre piece with music by David Burridge and book and lyrics by Martin Riley.
This engaging production was both an act of celebration and defiance: celebration of just what can be achieved when a community of performers forgets about professional or amateur status and simply co-operates in defiance of the dismal legacy of the Department of Education, who have done their best to crush any creativity in young people!

The Burning of the Boats tells the story of a Deal smuggling family and their plight when, in 1784 the then Prime Minister, William Pitt the younger, ordered the burning of boats on the beach in an attempt to eradicate illegal contraband. (I wonder what his solution to the current political situation would be?) The performance brought together a cast of fine actor/singers with children's choirs, adult choirs and the superb Revelation Strings with guest wind and percussion players. These huge forces were marshalled brilliantly by director Matthew Sharp and musical director David Burridge.

A sports hall is not necessarily the most sympathetic environment in which to stage a show but, in this case, it provided the size and sense of adventure for such an ambitious and varied production. On the central stage the compelling story was acted out with real sensitivity and focus and we were drawn into the desperate plight of the poor and the pathos of a pair of young lovers who preferred to flee for a better life than stay to perpetuate their families' illegal way of making a living. The strong, operatic moments were beautifully handled both vocally and theatrically.

Supporting the main action was the singing chorus: even though they had to contend with difficult acoustics and sightlines, they brought a richness and sense of vibrant musical colour to the performance and the playing of the orchestra was invariably exhilarating and dramatic. This was the second time that this cleverly crafted piece had public performances: its first appearance was at the Deal Festival a few years ago and it certainly deserves to be seen and heard over and over again. Such a celebration of the power of the arts to enrich lives has never been more needed nor more lovingly presented.

Teacher's notes

Once you have discussed the general impression that this review has had on your students you may well need to use some probing questions to discover what facts may be eluding both them and you. We might well ask 'what makes someone want to write a Musical?' Clearly there is always the possibility of commercial success but, in statistical terms, this is rare and so there are usually other motivating factors. In order to understand more about the creation of a new Musical we need to establish a context for its original writing and that is the purpose of the following section.

Stage two: Establishing context

Key facts: We list some useful information about The Burning of the Boats here:

1   Deal is a small town on the South East coast of the United Kingdom. The narrow stretch of ocean that separates it from France is known as 'The Downs' and there are treacherous sand banks lying off-shore.

2   Until the late nineteenth century, when the shingle deposits became excessive, Deal was a major mooring place for the British Navy and much of the commerce of the town was carried out by small boats ferrying goods and mariners back and forwards from the ships at anchor.

3   Deal once had more taverns, inns and drinking places than any other small town in England.

4   In recent years Deal not only lost its naval connections; it also lost its two other major sources of employment: the Royal Marines' School of Music (which provided highly skilled professional musicians to the armed forces) and a busy coal mine which extended some miles under the sea and was worked largely by miners who had migrated from the North of England.

5   Deal is now well-known as a weekend retreat for artists who have acquired and renovated attractive cottages in areas that were once 'run down' and inhabited by people (often fishermen and their families) with low incomes. Music halls, taverns, Mission halls and brothels have become fashionable places to live.

6   The composer of The Burning of the Boats is a graduate of the Royal Marines' School of Music and is now the musical director of

a project known as The Big Reveal, which specializes in bringing instrumental and vocal music to communities and young people in the South East of England. His orchestra is known as 'Revelation Strings'. David is highly skilled in composition and in arranging numbers from the rock/pop and classical worlds for performance by his orchestra and other groups of local musicians.

7   The writer, Martin Riley, is the grandson of a miner from the North of England and became fond of Deal when his Grandmother brought him to visit the town at holiday times. He has a profound knowledge of life in the 'pits', has written for television, directs a Theatre company and has published several stage works. He states in the credits for *The Burning of the Boats* that he not only wrote the libretto but the 'story' as well. This suggests that, although the Musical is clearly based on an actual historical event, the characters and what happens to them are fictional. Martin is typical of the multitalented 'creatives' who sustain live Theatre away from Broadway and the West End.

8   Deal now has its own Arts Festival, encouraging performances of drama, dance, music and poetry. This is where this work was first performed.

Task 2

Ask your students to study this list carefully and encourage them to make connections between the facts and the idea that a Musical was written as a result of some of them.

Teacher's notes
We might reasonably speculate that the writers were motivated by a desire to celebrate aspects of local culture and, perhaps, to introduce younger members of the performance company and audience to factors in the area's history. This 'local' dimension does not mean that the musical cannot be of wider interest: as we shall see when we investigate further, the Musical engages with universal themes. It is not necessary to live in Berlin to appreciate **Cabaret** nor in Paris to enjoy **Les Misérables**! In several senses this is a 'Community Musical'. Your research will show that there is a constant stream of such works which inspire generations of performers and creative artists. The work we see on Broadway or in any major theatrical city is the tip of a fascinating iceberg that rewards constant exploration.

Task 3

At this stage engage your students in a closer involvement with a scene from *The Burning of the Boats*. Ask them to re-read the review and understand the predicament of the two young lovers. We are providing the text and music for a scene that culminates in a sung duet between them together with substantial suggestions for an approach to working on this scene. The librettist provides comprehensive information about the various characters at the start of his text. Here is what he says about the two characters for our scene:

Jack Hagget, 18 years, Betsy's older brother

Jack can read and write and do figures because he's had some education paid for by his father so that he can do the accounts for the smuggling business. But he isn't excited by smuggling, which he sees as a dirty, dangerous, illegal, unromantic and potentially deadly trade that risks bringing the law and the military down on them. Jack is fond of his mother and Betsy but his pushy little brother, Sam, is a constant irritation to him and he's often at odds with his father, whom he knows wishes he was more of a 'man of action'. Jack's in love with Vicky Fishpole, which exasperates his father because there is only an uneasy working truce with the Fishpoles, who are seen as a rival clan and potential enemies. Jack wants Vicky and a different kind of life.

Vicky Fishpole, 17 years, Jack's beloved

Vicky is bullied by her rough and ready family, who have traditionally provided the muscle behind the smuggling business. She's intelligent and canny but has a bunch of brothers and boy cousins who rule the roost. Her life at home, like her mother's, is cooking and cleaning and ministering to the 'boys'. She has been expected to marry one of her cousins – brutes of lads who are into dog fighting, cock fighting and just about any kind of fighting – but she loves Jack because he is different. Vicky dreams of a future with him away from both their families.

Fly Away

Here, now, is a scene with a duet and chorus to explore. There is something for everyone!

Firstly, you should read the lyrics several times, and get a clear idea of what is actually going on at this moment in the narrative. This must be done whether you are playing the character of Jack, Vicky or a member of the ensemble. You are all as important as each other.

Now, let's break down the scene and see what is happening:

The original text of the scene	Ideas to explore in sections of the text
Onto the empty stage walks Jack, warily, with a lantern. He puts the lantern down and whistles. Vicky comes on behind him and hugs him. He winces. She lets go . . .	Chorus to sit in a circle providing enough space for some simple action to take place within the circle.

	Jack and Vicky must enter from different places through the circle and meet. Do not discuss how to play this scene, just do it! React to what happens only.
VICKY You're hurt. JACK I'd rather have the pain and you held me. *(taking her in his arms)* Hold me again. *They embrace for a moment and then Jack steps away to pick up the lantern*	Do the first acting exercise on *'You're Hurt'* with the response: *'I'm Hurt'* Repeat exercise with Jack *'I'd rather have the pain'* Vicky repeats *'You'd rather have the pain'* Now run the scene, repeating each line spoken before speaking your own line.
JACK Let me see your face. VICKY *(steps away and covers her face.)* No. JACK *(seeing, by the light of the lantern that her face is bruised)* It's you that's hurt. What have they . . . .?	**Repeat these three lines from memory.** *Taking alternate speaking parts, try to make the movements fit what is being said.* First time <u>Jack will say 'Let me See your face' and</u> <u>Vicky will say **'No'**.</u> When the three lines are repeated <u>Vicky will now say 'Let me See your face' and Jack will now say **'No'**</u>
VICKY I was late – with their meat – and my brothers said they'd seen us together. They hate you – and all your family – and I hate them. . . . *A beat. He puts his arm tenderly around her.* And I love you. JACK And I, you, Vicky. So, let's be done with hate – and be done with our families and their dirty business – and be done with this town: there's no free trade here for love and no hope of a future for you and me.	**At this point in the scene there will be some interesting things to note:** When repeating this sequence of words, what happens? Try to work out how this is dealt with by the speakers. What does it mean for your listening? Do they hear everything or only what they want to hear? Are they accurate in their repetition? If not, why not? What is actually happening between them?

VICKY
What'll we do?
JACK
We're young. Our life lies before us. Let's away together – to London, to marry – to seek our fortune!
(sings. Vicky joins in – and choir)
 	
When love must hide its face
Because of shame;
When lovers fear disgrace
To speak their name,
Then, like a songbird
In dawn's early light,
True love must spread its wings
And take to flight.
 	
Fly away, my true love, with me.
Fly away, far away with me.
Like birds in search of better
   weather,
Fly away where we can live
A life of love, together;
Away, love, forever, with me.
 	
When dark suspicions breed
In every heart;
When jealousy and greed
Drive love apart,
Like birds in the autumn
Flying South and West,
True lovers know it's time
To leave the nest.
 	
Fly away, my true love, with me.
Fly away, far away with me.
Like birds in search of better
   weather,
Fly away where we can live
A life of love, together;
Away, love, forever, with me.
Away, love, forever, with me.
	Please see all notes below for this section of the text.

VICKY I would go now – you know I would. But how shall we live?	Complete the 'repetition exercise' with this text as you did in the opening section.
JACK I can read and write; I could try for a clerk. But we shall need some money in our purse, or we'll have no hope.	Both characters must repeat what they hear before speaking their own lines.
VICKY My father would rather cut his throat than give me a penny.	Try not to look at the words of the script when you speak. Put the book down each time you speak. It doesn't matter if you speak the lines in small sections to start with. You will improve as time goes on.
JACK Mine would cut my throat and yours if he knew of this. But he doesn't – so bide your time and let me consider. Listen out for me, tomorrow, through the wall – and come when I whistle.	Make notes and observations on what happened and talk about it with the company.

Task 4

Performance notes for duet & chorus

Consider all the ideas which were discussed in the chapter on chorus and how you can make the narrative come alive. Who are you? Are you watching the action or are you part of the action? How do you relate to each other? Are you all of 'one mind' or are their opportunities for conflict to be utilized in the playing of the chorus parts?

Look at the narrative of the scene and try to work out exactly what is going on and where the plot is going. Remember our image of a map and the directions that enabled you to get to your destination? In the same way this scene has a set of directions which the cast must recognize and follow in order to realize its dramatic potential.

Some questions to ask when investigating the **map of the scene's narrative:**

Opening of scene

- The chorus are present and are watching the action. Where were they before?
- What is the purpose of the chorus? To listen, comment or be part of the action?
- Are the chorus the reason why Jack and Vicky arrive on the scene?

Entry of Jack and Vicky

- Do Jack and Vicky think they are on their own at the start of the scene?
- When do they realize that the chorus exists?
- Entry of Jack. Where from? Where is he going? Is he looking for Vicky?
- Entry of Vicky. Where from? Where is she going? Is she looking for Jack?
- Who sees who first and what is the reaction?
- How do they deal with the 'hurt' and 'pain'?
- Their need to escape needs to be at the back of their minds during the opening moments of this scene.

Musical number 'Fly Away': opening sequence

- As the song begins the time sequence slows down. How does this impact upon the physicality of both Jack and Vicky? What ideas might you have for these moments?
- There is no pressure or urgency for a moment. How will these eventually be communicated to the audience?

Musical number 'Fly Away': middle section

- What are the chorus doing during the opening dramatic sequence of action and the first section of the duet?
- Who knows who is present on stage?
- Do Jack and Vicky think they are still on their own when they are singing to each other?

Musical number 'Fly Away': final section

- Do they ever address the chorus at any time during the song?
- How do Jack and Vicky react when the chorus starts to comment upon their situation?
- How does the duet resolve itself?
- What happens to the chorus as characters within the narrative after the song has finished?
- Was it all a dream and Jack and Vicky always on their own?

End of scene

- How would you stage the ending of this scene?
- Do both Jack and Vicky leave in the same way as they came on stage? If not, why not?
- Do they leave at the same time?
- Does one character watch the other go first? If so why? What is the implication of this action? What does it say about the narrative and intention of the character?
- Do the chorus remain? If not, why do they leave? What is their motivation to leave?

You might think: too many questions?
The more you ask the better your work will become. The process is all important and the conversation is part of that all-important process. The process is what really matters, not the final performance.

Task 5

Opening of scene

Before looking at the song the scene needs to be set. It might be useful to do a simple exercise with the opening dialogue to see how this impacts upon the entire company.
The two characters should sit opposite each other, and the chorus should sit in a circle around them. This will mean that all the chorus are watching the two players from different angles. They are not seeing the same things. The task is for the chorus to observe every movement and facial gesture and to see how these impact upon them as both the storytellers and the audience. What do they see and feel? How does that make each of them feel about the two characters?

What then happens is this!
Vicky looks at the script and then puts the script down and speaks her line from memory 'You're hurt.'

Jack looks straight at Vicky and, having heard the line, repeats it, changing the personal pronoun to 'I'm hurt.'

This must be repeated over and over again exactly as you hear it in order to see what happens between the two actors. When it is the right moment (after about the twentieth time and the laughter has stopped) you will need to discuss these moments and talk about them with the rest of the company. What did they see or what did they feel and when, at what point, did something change?

Then try it the other way around with Jack saying '*I'd rather have the pain*' and Vicky replies, staring straight at Jack, '*You'd rather have the pain.*'

Do exactly the same thing, trying to repeat the words as you heard them, although you will change the personal pronoun; e.g. 'I' becomes 'you'.

Teacher's notes
Repeat the exercise with other members of the chorus so that they all get the opportunity to explore this work and see what they observe. You could ask everyone in the class to try this so that they all experience it. Don't be disheartened: this sometimes doesn't work but it is a chance to go from the unknown to see what happens! Something magical can sometimes occur. We cannot tell you what!

Having explored these few lines for this scene. We would suggest that you take the whole scene and engage in a listening exercise.

Task 6

Each character speaks their line. The other actor looks them in the eyes and repeats the line as accurately as they have heard it. They then speak their own line and the other character repeats the lines heard before speaking their next line. Each time you speak, try not to look at the script. Look at the script first and then speak the line. It doesn't matter how slow the process is.

Again, and very importantly, discuss the findings with everyone and see what the chorus members observed.

This exercise should be done several times so that there is a sense of freedom about the emotional content of the scene. Let it happen rather than deciding what should happen! Stop controlling the scene; let it take its own course.

It would be useful to repeat this first section several times and see what changes with each version. Write these observations down and discuss them with each other and the rest of the chorus. What the chorus hear and see is particularly important.

Task 7

Duet and Chorus 'Fly Away'

We focus on the lyrics first to see what happens. Look at the lyrics in the libretto and not in the musical score.

Give your students the following guidance:
Each character should read their lines in a normal voice and at a normal speed. Do not (i) try to find a rhythm (ii) place any emotional feeling or inflections into the text (iii) try to work out what it means to each of you. Just speak the text.

Take no notice of the punctuation; just speak the words as they come to you and as you feel them. Let the words happen as they are sounded!

You might notice that when you start speaking the same words together at 'Then like a song bird ...' you will take breaths at different times; you will speak at different tempi. Don't worry: this is what happens in real life. It is also what happens in the score of the Musical. You could try to speak it together, looking at each other very closely as you speak. See what happens. Is somebody waiting for the other or is it a genuine sense of 'togetherness'? Does it matter? What do you discover? Talk about it?

Both characters should speak their lyrics up to the entry of the chorus as a monologue in order to discover what the words mean to them as individuals. When speaking the lyric as an individual, allow the character to decide their setting and be secure in every detail. Work out what makes you speak the first words.

Ask the question: *Where does my energy come from to speak these words?*

Once you have decided upon the answer to this question, find a 'trigger' that sets this emotional response in action. Find a key word that does the trick and helps you remember the setting you have decided upon. You must always know why the words are being spoken. In this case why are they often being spoken as one voice (together)?

Food for thought

You might also notice that the words of Vicky when she first speaks are the same as Jack's. Have you ever had a conversation when your sentences are finished by someone else? How does that make you feel? Does it annoy you that you can't complete your thought or alternatively are you relieved that someone thinks the same as you? How do we deal with that emotion in this lyric? Is this a sign of '*togetherness*' on a completely different level? Perhaps the 'taking flight' is the clue. It is not a human experience to have wings and take flight and yet it is the desire of us all to be as 'free as a bird'!

Task 8

Points to think about and discuss when rehearsing and performing this first section of the musical number 'Fly Away'.

Jack sings alone the following lyrics:

When love must hide its face
Because of shame;
When lovers fear disgrace
To speak their name

Jack is clearly establishing a situation and a problem to be solved with the repetition of the word '*when*'. This clearly refers to time and for a potential set of actions to be followed. What might these actions be?

At this point Vicky joins in and continues with Jack's thinking by suggesting that both are aware of what should happen as a consequence:

Then, like a songbird
In dawn's early light,
True love must spread its wings
And take to flight.

This togetherness of thought is purely magical and we have to believe that something happens to them to enable them to synchronize their thinking. How are you to achieve this?

The next section is more of a conversation and whilst one (Vicky) is enjoying the idea of the concept of being able to 'fly', Jack is moving the action onwards by asking Vicky to fly away with him. This sequence of question and answer is significant but is soon completed by a return to the universality of their relationship by their singing:

Like birds in search of better weather,

At this point the music changes and the compound time of 6/8 is significant because it heightens the magical quality of flying as both melodies move gradually upwards as if reaching for the sky.

Fly away where we can live:

returning to the dependable time signature of 4/4 as the melody once more descends to the earth from the sky.

A life of love, together; Away, love, forever, with me.

At this point the music reverts to the beginning introductory music. Once more we are allowed to enter the world of the characters but there must now be a sense of the narrative being told by the spectators – the Chorus.

When the members of the ensemble join together to tell their part of the story, they sing the same words and the same melody 'as one voice' (unison) thus strengthening the message and identifying the universality of the narrative. The words sung are as follows:

When dark suspicions breed
In every heart;
When jealousy and greed
Drive love apart,
Like birds in the autumn
Flying South and West,
True lovers know it's time

Then a magical moment occurs when the voices split and in 3-part harmony enjoy the final phrase:

To leave the nest.

The final chorus is a celebration and affirmation that the decision must be to:

Fly away where we can live
A life of love, together;
Away, love, forever, with me.
Away, love, forever, with me.

The Burning of the Boats

7. Fly Away (Duet Jack and Vicky)

Copyright - David Burridge/Martin Riley (2013)

2

V.S.

4

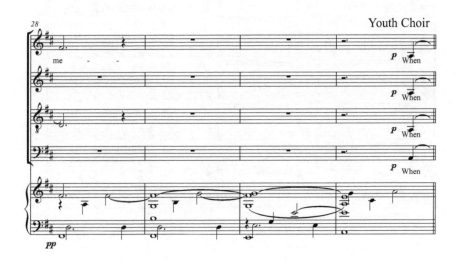

5

6

All these moments in the scene need to be understood as part of the narrative. All members of the chorus and each performer must be aware of their contribution to the overall consequences and narrative being explored. What they are singing and doing must have a sense of purpose to bring truth to the action and validity to the performance work.

Some exciting adventures are to be had in discovering how to tell this story. To create this scene and bring the magic to each dramatic event is in your hands. Enjoy the challenge!

Teacher's notes

This beautiful song is one of the high points in the drama and demonstrates that memorable musical moments are not confined to better-known Musicals. As students prepare their performances with the exercises we have provided and then move on to learn the music they must bear in mind all the material we have provided in earlier lessons. They will need to explore the best tempo and dynamics for the piece together with acquiring total accuracy in tuning and phrasing. All these technical qualities will support the underlying interaction between the two characters and enable an audience to sense their communication, aspirations and fears. It is a moment well worth developing and sharing.

A Final Note

In his autobiography *Unmasked* (2018), the composer Andrew Lloyd Webber speaks of: 'that rare moment when the planets, Casting, Book, Music, Lyrics, Chorography and Design align.' We hope that we have provided the potential for your students to experience this because, as Lloyd Webber says, 'It is a reminder of how incredibly collaborative and fragile that process is' (p.482).

Topics for class discussion, student journal entries or essay assignments

1 If you were to write a new Musical what topic would you select?
2 Research the extent of new Musicals featuring in your town or city and note the size and scope of the production.
3 What was the emotional impact of the sung duet from *The Burning of the Boats*?
4 What performance notes would you give to the actors for the scene which culminates in the duet you have studied in this lesson?
5 If you were to write a Musical would you use dialogue or have the piece 'sung through'? What would be the basis of your decision?

6 Write a new scene in which you show Jack and Vicky in their future life.

7 Find a duet from any other Musical and write an analysis of what is happening in order to help performers working on the scene.

8 Why has the Musical become such a popular form of Theatre?

9 What events in your own country's history would make a good Musical?

10 How have organizations behind major productions ensured the financial success of their Musicals?

SAMPLE TEST QUESTIONS (MULTIPLE CHOICE)

1 *The Burning of the Boats* is set in the: a) seventeenth century b) twentieth century c) eighteenth century d) fifteenth century.

2 The writers of *The Burning of the Boats* were mainly inspired by: a) A commission b) A need to make money c) Local knowledge d) The idea of reaching the West End.

3 Many Musicals do not reach Broadway or the West End because: a) They are written for a specific community b) They lack quality c) There is no single 'hit' song d) The cast is too big.

4 Even though the setting of *The Burning of the Boats* is a specific location in Southern England, it would be of interest to a wider audience because: a) It deals with some universal themes b) It focuses on local history c) It contains lively dialogue d) It has memorable tunes.

5 When you are preparing a duet for performance you must first establish: a) The melody b) The exact words of the text c) What is really going on between the characters d) The key in which the music is written.

6 When a Musical involves dialogue it is essential to: a) Speak with the right accent b) Move easily between speaking and singing c) Speak as loudly as you sing d) Learn the words quickly.

7 Writing a Musical usually involves two people but some Musicals have been written by a single person. Examples include: a) Leonard Bernstein b) Arthur Sullivan c) Stephen Sondheim d) Tim Rice.

8 *The Burning of the Boats*, like many other works of Musical Theatre, is based on: a) A legend b) A fiction c) A well-known poem d) A true, historical event.

9 When there is a chorus in a Musical it is now recognized that they are: a) Of minor interest to the audience b) Of equal importance to any other characters c) Best not seen d) Spectators.

10 *Cabaret* is an example of a Musical with a very precise historical and physical setting in: a) Twentieth century Paris b) 1940s New York c) 1930s Berlin d) 1950s London.

Reflection: Lesson Twelve – Making your own Musical

Having considered a completely new piece of Musical Theatre in this final lesson, it might be appropriate for you to create a Musical with your students. In the same way that you would bake a cake you now have all the ingredients for this task. All you need to do is to throw down the gauntlet, engage with your students and be creative.

One form which will prove popular with your students is the **Jukebox Musical** and we would suggest the following plan for creating your own example.

First, identify exactly what a 'Jukebox' Musical is. (Remember that they, and possibly you, are not familiar with jukeboxes in coffee bars and pubs!) We suggest that you introduce them to the work of ABBA and the film of the Musical 'Mamma Mia' or the music of Queen in 'We Will Rock You'. Other artists who have been associated with this form of Musical include The Temptations, Cher, Carole King, Jersey Boys, and Michael Jackson. Let your students identify the repertoire of an artist they would like to investigate.

Once they have chosen the artist, ask your students to select six songs to explore in some detail. Factors to consider when choosing the repertoire include contrasting moods, different qualities of lyric and the narrative, personal and, possibly, didactic aspects of the songs. Having selected the six songs, your students should start to consider the structure of the piece of Musical Theatre by putting the songs in order so that there is a strong song at the beginning and either a repeat of the opening or another strong song at the end. This will create the climax and final curtain of your Musical. This is an opportunity to remind your students of all the points they discovered in the lesson about the book, the lyrics and music.

Having decided the order of the songs, identify what each song is about. The next stage is to build a short narrative description of the content and meaning of each song. When your students have completed this task, discuss a potential linking theme arising from the lyrics. Often, when working with the output of one specific artist, it is possible to detect a theme underlying many of the songs and you can construct a narrative between one song and the next. The aim is to build a story that links the music together and to tell a story using newly created characters.

Now your students have a choice *either* to tell the story through the music and create a 'through composed Musical' like *Les Misérables* or *Miss Saigon* or create a Musical with some dialogue between each song in a similar style to many of the Musicals they have already studied.

The main object is to create a set of songs which are to be linked with a narrative. This will provide your students with the opportunity to work with familiar material. The linking sections of dialogue should initially be improvised and spoken by the identified characters. This will create a smooth transit between one song and the next. However, you could also encourage your students to rewrite the lyrics to create a new narrative. Remember: this is a Musical created by your students. There are no rules to be broken. Only a Musical to be created!

Solo songs have the potential to be made into duets by sharing the lyric and a song can be sung by many people to create a chorus. The choice is for the students engaged in the creative process. This is an opportunity for them to explore their own experience of music and bring it into the world of Musical Theatre through dialogue, action and physical gestures. It might be helpful preparation to look at Musicals on film built around a single artist, such as:

Moulin Rouge (2001)

The Blues Brothers (1980)

Singin' In The Rain (1952)

Saturday Night Fever (1977)

It is wise to use an uncomplicated setting which is relatively easy to assemble. You will probably have a set of boxes in your green room which could be arranged into different shapes to provide varying heights to indicate specific locations. Try to engage with the audience's imagination. Keep it simple and let your short Musical tell its own story. All too often performances are cluttered up with the 'glitter' of commercialism and overtly excessive technical demands take over from the message being expressed.

The beauty of this work is that the songs chosen will often have backing tracks available online and so a built-in orchestra is available to enhance the students' final performance. You will not need to engage the music department to orchestrate the Musical: just invite them to the show.

We are convinced that, if these studies culminate in enabling your students to create their own Musical, you will have taken them on a journey they will never forget.

Have fun.

ANSWERS TO SAMPLE TEST QUESTIONS

Please note that there may be more than one correct answer to the questions.

Lesson One:
1. c); 2. d); 3.b); 4. a) or c); 5. b); 6. b); 7. d); 8. b); 9. b); 10. b)

Lesson Two:
1. d); 2. c); 3. a); 4. b); 5. a); 5. c); 7. b); 8. b); 9. a); 10.b)

Lesson Three:
1. b); 2. a); 3. c); 4. b); 5. d); 6. b); 7. c); 8. b); 9. b. 10. b)

Lesson Four:
1. c); 2. c); 3. c); 4. a) and c); 5. c); 6. a); 7. a), c) and d); 8. b) 9. a) and b); 10. b)

Lesson Five:
1. c); 2. b); 3. a); 4. c); 5. c. 6. b); 7. c); 8. b); 9. b); 10. b)

Lesson Six:
1. b); 2. c); 3. a); 4. c); 5. b); 6. c); 7. d); 8. c); 9. d); 10. b)

Lesson Seven:
1. b); 2. c); 3. b); 4. d); 5. a); 6. c); 7. d); 8. c); 9. d); 10. c)

Lesson Eight:
1. b); 2. d); 3. c); 4. b); 5. b); 6. c); 7. b); 8. c); 9. c); 10. c)

Lesson Nine:
1. b); 2. c); 3. d); 4. b); 5. c); 6. c); 7. b); 8. d); 9. a); 10. c)

Lesson Ten:
1. b); 2. c); 3. c); 4. a); 5. d); 6. c); 7. d); 8. a) and d); 9. b); 10. b)

Lesson Eleven:
1. c); 2. b); 3. c); 4. a); 5. b); 6. c); 7. a); 8. b); 9. b); 10. c)

Lesson Twelve:
1. c); 2. c); 3. a); 4. a); 5. c); 6. b); 7. c); 8. d); 9. b); 10. c)

SOURCES AND RESOURCES

The following sources have either been used in the compiling of these lessons or will provide further help for teachers.

Books providing historical and critical views

Bogard, T. et al. (Eds.) *The Revels History of Drama in English. Vol.viii, American Drama*. London: Methuen. 1977.
Established the vital contribution of the American Musical to world drama.

Burden, M. et al. (Eds.) *Staging History 1780–1840*. Oxford: The Bodlean Library. 2016.
A rich and fascinating source of information about the early days of Musical Theatre.

Ganzl, Kurt. *Musicals: The complete illustrated story of the world's most popular live entertainment*. London: Carlton. 1995.
An attractive and well-illustrated account of the rise of Musical Theatre but a somewhat irritating 'jokey' tone from the author.

Guernsey, Otis L. (Ed.) *Playwrights, Lyricists, Composers on Theater*. New York: Dodd, Mead and Company. 1974.
After many years this remains a rich source of information about the relationship between writers and composers.

Harwood, R. *All the World's a Stage*. London: Methuen. 1984.
Although this was published many years ago the Chapter entitled 'Razzmatazz and Realism' remains one of the best written descriptions of the emergence of the American Musical.

Lloyd Webber, Andrew. *Unmasked: A memoir*. London: Harper Collins. 2018.
An inspirational account of the work of a highly successful creator of Musicals, providing insights into the collaboration with writers, choreographers and designers.

Powell, K. (Ed.) *The Cambridge Companion to Victorian and Edwardian Theatre*. Cambridge: Cambridge University Press. 2004.
Fascinating information about the role of music in Theatre and the roots of the Musical.

Schino, M. *An Indra's Web: The Age of Appia, Craig, Stanislavski, Meyerhold, Copeau, Artaud*. Wroclow: Icarus. 2018.
A rich source of ideas and inspiration.

Sondheim, S. *Finishing the Hat: Collected Lyrics (1954–1981)*. London: Virgin. 1981.
Provides wonderful insights into the process of writing lyrics.

Taylor, M. and Symonds, D. *Studying Musical Theatre: Theory and Practice*. London: Palgrave. 2014.
Establishes clear principles for critical thinking about the subject.

Practical handbooks

Casado, D. *Teaching Musical Theatre: The Essential Handbook*. New York: Beat by Beat. 2017.
Lively ideas for 7–14-year-old students.

de Mallet Burgess, T. and Skilbeck, N. *The Singing and Acting Handbook: Games and exercises for the performer*. London and New York: Routledge. 2000.
A useful resource book once you have established sound ways of working.

Gilbert, C. (2019) *The SAVI Singing Actor: Your guide to peak performance on the Musical Stage*. www.savisingingactor.com

Henson, D. and Pickering, K. *Musical Theatre: A workbook*. London: Red Globe. 2013

Henson, D. and Pickering, K. *Musical Theatre: A further workbook*. London: Red Globe. 2017.
These three books provide extensive practical guidance by establishing a dialogue with students.

Sunderland, M. and Pickering, K. *Choreographing the Stage Musical*. Studio City: Players Press. 2008.
Packed with suggestions for inexperienced choreographers.

Tebbutt, Gerry. *Musical Theatre Handbook*. London: Dramatic Lines. 2003.
Particularly useful for those preparing for auditions.

Works cited

For information on *The Burning Of The Boats* contact: *Norman North at The Agency (London) Ltd 24 Pottery Lane London W11 4LZ*. Tel: *020 7727 1346* Fax: *020 7727 903*.
http://www.theagency.co.uk

Corp, Hal. *The Great American Songbook*. New York: 2007.
The Great American Songbook is the canon of approximately 459 of the most important and influential American popular songs. Often referred to as 'Jazz' or 'American' standards from the Golden Age of popular music between the 1920s and 1950s, these songs have been performed by many famous artists. The music has been associated with Broadway and its love affair with Musical Theatre and the Film Musicals of Hollywood.

MUSICAL THEATRE: ONLINE RESOURCES

Music Hall History	https://www.youtube.com/watch?v=UU2rRyc0X8Q&t=4653s	1 hr 30 mins
Vaudeville	https://www.youtube.com/watch?v=vNTbJi8rc1Q&list=PLrbaoKBy-cP1hMsZg8mgCLbjSB3u6tp0O&index=33	2 hrs

The Story of Musicals (Part 1)	https://www.youtube.com/watch?v=bBjntZmrxg0&t=1s	20 mins
The Story of Musicals (Part 2)	https://www.youtube.com/watch?v=0fjC0iMMtqE	25 mins
The Story of Musicals (Part 3)	https://www.youtube.com/watch?v=yyXOhV4dIxQ	15 mins
The Story of Musicals (Part 4)	https://www.youtube.com/watch?v=a5pD3iO7H_o	18 mins
The Story of Musicals (Part 5)	https://www.youtube.com/watch?v=yzQs27B9jkl	19 mins
The Story of Musicals (Part 6)	https://www.youtube.com/watch?v=AVms-Um-SPY&list=PL295D58F11AB4DB65&index=6	21 mins
The Story of Musicals (Part 7)	https://www.youtube.com/watch?v=JIU6eyaM4Lk&list=PL295D58F11AB4DB65&index=7	19 mins
The Story of Musicals (Part 8)	https://www.youtube.com/watch?v=8wy7CmBXJ8k&list=PL295D58F11AB4DB65&index=8	22 mins
The Story of Musicals (Part 9)	https://www.youtube.com/watch?v=Z2Nxn7H5YqM&list=PL295D58F11AB4DB65&index=9	17 mins

Broadway: The American Musical EP1:1	https://www.youtube.com/watch?v=nPtAKdGZYt0&list=PLDolR_yYiQsKuPBiM7H29GOFOXo7G-ogG&index=1	21 mins

Broadway: The American Musical EP1:2	https://www.youtube.com/watch?v=N-y2EYGR6SI&list=PLDoIR_yYiQsKuPBiM7H29GOFOXo7G-ogG&index=2	24 mins
Broadway: The American Musical EP1:3	https://www.youtube.com/watch?v=PnmKixojKgs&list=PLDoIR_yYiQsKuPBiM7H29GOFOXo7G-ogG&index=3	12 mins
Broadway: The American Musical EP2:1	https://www.youtube.com/watch?v=EFw0Xwfk0EI&list=PLDoIR_yYiQsKuPBiM7H29GOFOXo7G-ogG&index=4	24 mins
Broadway: The American Musical EP2:2	https://www.youtube.com/watch?v=_uPSAFdp_XA&list=PLDoIR_yYiQsKuPBiM7H29GOFOXo7G-ogG&index=5	22 mins
Broadway: The American Musical EP2:3	https://www.youtube.com/watch?v=YVuWjT7V7h0&list=PLDoIR_yYiQsKuPBiM7H29GOFOXo7G-ogG&index=6	11 mins
Broadway: The American Musical EP3:1	https://www.youtube.com/watch?v=0AQcstcR6Dw&list=PLDoIR_yYiQsKuPBiM7H29GOFOXo7G-ogG&index=7	23 mins
Broadway: The American Musical EP3:2	https://www.youtube.com/watch?v=ieRjKcN4yZY&list=PLgMP8eFmGggedv1vMxDnTFC6XA5fenRTY&index=8	22 mins
Broadway: The American Musical EP3:3	https://www.youtube.com/watch?v=T_BF2jWcE4A&list=PLgMP8eFmGggedv1vMxDnTFC6XA5fenRTY&index=9	11 mins
Broadway: The American Musical EP4:1	https://www.youtube.com/watch?v=ffDBgjpIOlg&list=PLgMP8eFmGggedv1vMxDnTFC6XA5fenRTY&index=10	23 mins
Broadway: The American Musical EP4:2	https://www.youtube.com/watch?v=Kj2VjZam_lo&list=PLgMP8eFmGggedv1vMxDnTFC6XA5fenRTY&index=11	21 mins
Broadway: The American Musical EP4:3	https://www.youtube.com/watch?v=La2m_uoGEQI&list=PLgMP8eFmGggedv1vMxDnTFC6XA5fenRTY&index=12	13 mins
Broadway: The American Musical EP5:1	https://www.youtube.com/watch?v=Rg_SRV8WLH4&list=PLgMP8eFmGggedv1vMxDnTFC6XA5fenRTY&index=13	23 mins

Broadway: The American Musical EP5:2	https://www.youtube.com/watch?v=7ZfJBQPv1aU&list=PLgMP8eFmGggedv1vMxDnTFC6XA5fenRTY&index=14	23 mins
Broadway: The American Musical EP5:3	https://www.youtube.com/watch?v=roi6q2muhys&list=PLgMP8eFmGggedv1vMxDnTFC6XA5fenRTY&index=15	12 mins
Broadway: The American Musical EP6:1	https://www.youtube.com/watch?v=ERzGdKymvdM&list=PLgMP8eFmGggedv1vMxDnTFC6XA5fenRTY&index=16	23 mins
Broadway: The American Musical EP6:2	https://www.youtube.com/watch?v=3EDzxWH-nuc&list=PLgMP8eFmGggedv1vMxDnTFC6XA5fenRTY&index=17	22 mins
Broadway: The American Musical EP6:3	https://www.youtube.com/watch?v=fY8Qlix07ok&list=PLgMP8eFmGggedv1vMxDnTFC6XA5fenRTY&index=18	13 mins

Taboo – Documentary	https://www.youtube.com/watch?v=j8l3C3lPjn0&list=PLrbaoKBy-cP1hMsZg8mgCLbjSB3u6tp0O&index=11	48 mins
Andrew Lloyd Webber	https://www.youtube.com/watch?v=JQs3xyHnwdo&list=PLrbaoKBy-cP1hMsZg8mgCLbjSB3u6tp0O&index=12	1 hr 17 mins
One More Step – A Chorus Line	https://www.youtube.com/watch?v=5pzLPpvdorM&list=PLrbaoKBy-cP1hMsZg8mgCLbjSB3u6tp0O&index=16	1 hr 12 mins
Making of London '*Chicago*'	https://www.youtube.com/watch?v=Fpp-sbtxRyk&list=PLrbaoKBy-cP1hMsZg8mgCLbjSB3u6tp0O&index=17	57 mins
Les Misérables – Stage by Stage	https://www.youtube.com/watch?v=DHF4IW6xQil&list=PLrbaoKBy-cP1hMsZg8mgCLbjSB3u6tp0O&index=20	57 mins
The Lionel Bart Story	https://www.youtube.com/watch?v=uuwICEQnq88&list=PLrbaoKBy-cP1hMsZg8mgCLbjSB3u6tp0O&index=26	1 hr
Pride of *Lion King*	https://www.youtube.com/watch?v=5bLD2gZhmoU&list=PLrbaoKBy-cP1hMsZg8mgCLbjSB3u6tp0O&index=30	40 mins
French Musical Theatre	https://www.youtube.com/watch?v=vmjq93mEeU4&list=PLrbaoKBy-cP1hMsZg8mgCLbjSB3u6tp0O&index=34	1 hr 20 mins

The Making of *West Side Story*	https://www.youtube.com/watch?v=j3SEW63 LsaM&list=PLrbaoKBy-cP1hMsZg8mgCLbjSB3 u6tp0O&index=37	1 hr 30 mins
Evita: Making a Superstar	https://www.youtube.com/watch?v=H_YeBu8c3ho	58 mins
Phantom Of The Opera: Behind the Mask	https://www.youtube.com/watch?v=rpVTAvazjpg &list=PLBqWP6pXldAVNeary5wfsuli7F5DwtG _i&index=9	1 hr 30 mins
Imagine – Cameron Mackintosh: The Musical Man	https://www.youtube.com/watch?v=a6WlWKjilU4	1 hr 28 mins
The Witches of Eastwick (Part 1)	https://www.youtube.com/watch?v=UW7Roticth8	22 mins
The Witches of Eastwick (Part 2)	https://www.youtube.com/watch?v=in5C7-8-G9Q	20 mins
The Witches of Eastwick (Part 3)	https://www.youtube.com/watch?v=qGC02bOtzhM	10 mins
Stephen Sondheim (Part 1)	https://www.youtube.com/watch?v=Pa646nfBe Y8&list=PLAEA11276ED0E7645	6 mins
Stephen Sondheim (Part 2)	https://www.youtube.com/watch?v=uC0K1Ka_ jyk&list=PLAEA11276ED0E7645&index=2	10 mins
Stephen Sondheim (Part 3)	https://www.youtube.com/watch?v=6ldcHvDPa- c&list=PLAEA11276ED0E7645&index=3	6 mins
Stephen Sondheim (Part 4)	https://www.youtube.com/watch?v=Y1QisK_ jD40&list=PLAEA11276ED0E7645&index=4	5 mins
Stephen Sondheim (Part 5)	https://www.youtube.com/watch?v=ap36rjUpOAQ &list=PLAEA11276ED0E7645&index=5	6 mins
Stephen Sondheim (Part 6)	https://www.youtube.com/watch?v=FNX-Z_ jRpSk&list=PLAEA11276ED0E7645&index=6	5 mins
Stephen Sondheim (Part 7)	https://www.youtube.com/watch?v=GQS2b8 vHekw&list=PLAEA11276ED0E7645&index=7	7 mins
Company Documentary	https://www.youtube.com/watch?v=FDIO4fZC6Tg	53 mins
Great Performances: Hamilton's America	https://www.youtube.com/watch?v=SDTmlTgsye8	1 hr 24 mins